CW00496034

SPOOKY

Florida

Also in the Spooky Series by S. E. Schlosser
and Paul G. Hoffman:

Spooky California

Spooky Campfire Tales

Spooky Canada

Spooky Maryland

Spooky Massachusetts

Spooky Michigan

Spooky Montana

Spooky New England

Spooky New Jersey

Spooky New York

Spooky North Carolina

Spooky Oregon

Spooky Pennsylvania

Spooky South

Spooky Southwest

Spooky Texas

Spooky Virginia

Spooky Washington

Spooky Wisconsin

SPOOKY
Florida

*Tales of Hauntings, Strange Happenings,
and Other Local Lore*

RETOLD BY S. E. SCHLOSSER

ILLUSTRATED BY PAUL G. HOFFMAN

Guilford, Connecticut

Text copyright © 2010 by S. E. Schlosser
Illustrations copyright © 2010 by Paul G. Hoffman

Project editor: David Legere
Text design/layout: Lisa Reneson, Two Sisters Design
Map: M.A. Dubé © Rowman & Littlefield

Library of Congress Cataloging-in-Publication Data is available on file.

ISBN 978-0-7627-5122-8

Printed in the United States of America

For my family: David, Dena, Tim, Arlene, Hannah, Emma, Nathan, Ben, Deb, Gabe, Clare, Jack, Chris, Karen, Davey, and Aunt Mil.

For Tony Bustamante. Many thanks for your help.

For Erin Turner, Paul Hoffman, and all the wonderful folks at Globe Pequot Press, with my thanks.

For Loyd and Mildred Schlosser, who lived in and loved Florida. Love you, Grandma and Grandpa!

Contents

PART TWO: POWERS OF DARKNESS AND LIGHT

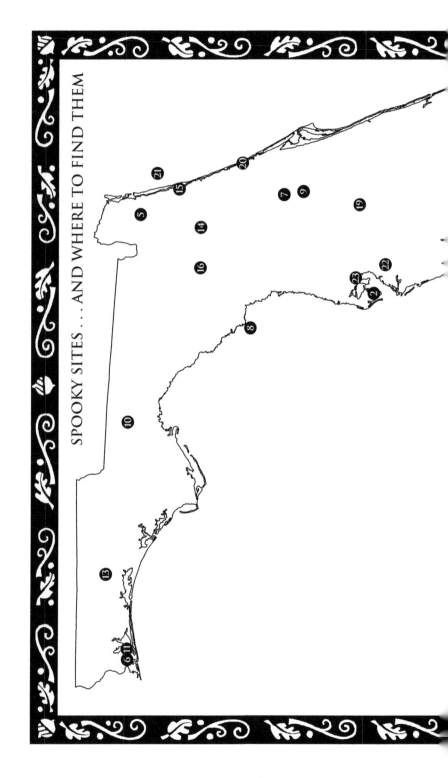

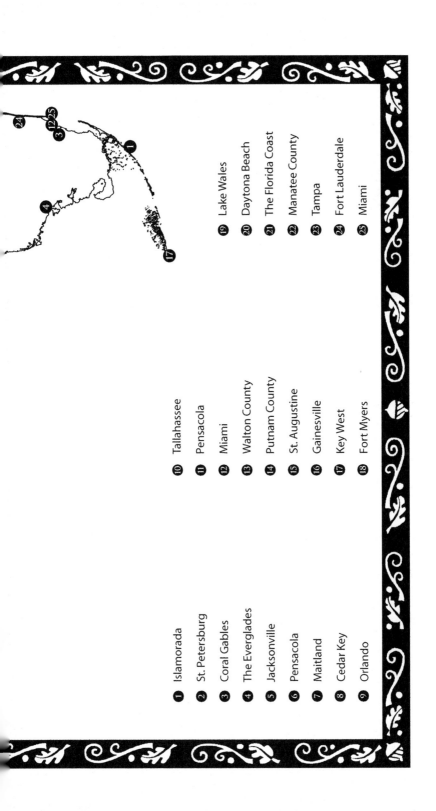

1 Islamarada
2 St. Petersburg
3 Coral Gables
4 The Everglades
5 Jacksonville
6 Pensacola
7 Maitland
8 Cedar Key
9 Orlando

10 Tallahassee
11 Pensacola
12 Miami
13 Walton County
14 Putnam County
15 St. Augustine
16 Gainesville
17 Key West
18 Fort Myers

19 Lake Wales
20 Daytona Beach
21 The Florida Coast
22 Manatee County
23 Tampa
24 Fort Lauderdale
25 Miami

Introduction

I was up at dawn on the last day of my Florida research trip and hurried out to Highway 1 with camera in hand. If the Islamorada ghost car (*The Antique Car*) appeared, I was determined to document it. No deal. The wind caressed my cheeks, bringing the scent of salt water with it. Two brown pelicans flew overhead and disappeared behind a screen of palm trees. Still no ghost car.

Sighing, I shouldered my SLR and headed back toward the hotel to pack up my bag. On the way, I was sidetracked by a gorgeous sunrise over the Atlantic and spent several minutes laughing at the antics of five seagulls perched on the wings of a water plane. How could I go back to snowy New York after all of this!

After a quick breakfast, I pointed the car north toward Miami and the Everglades. On my last day, I had decided to visit the Miccosukee Reservation and take one more airboat ride through the grassy river that is the Everglades, though on this trip I probably would not make it to the spot where Flight 401 went down in 1972, leaving behind wreckage and a bevy of ghosts. Still, it was a lovely warm day, and ghosts or not, I was determined to enjoy it.

First stop, the re-created Miccosukee village. As I strolled through the exhibits, I was drawn to a crowded theater facing a pen containing water, a bit of sandy beach, and a heck of a lot of big alligators. Oh boy! I watched in amazement as a

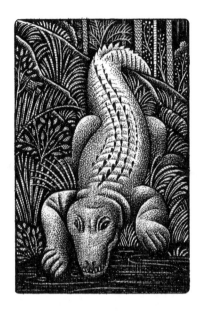

man from the tribe pulled an alligator out of the water by its tail (which doesn't hurt them) and wrestled with it. According to his explanation, alligators—once a food staple of the tribe—had to be brought home alive or their meat would spoil. This practice resulted in a series of moves that is today called alligator wrestling.

As the man performed amazing feats with a very large alligator, I pondered on another Native American who long ago fought an eighteen-foot rogue alligator that was exterminating the people in his village, one by one (*Spook Hill*). In the ensuing fight, a huge crater was created; it later filled with water and became a lake. That was some awesome gator wrestling!

After the gator-wrestling exhibition, I got to meet the tribesman and hold a baby gator in my hands. For several minutes the baby gator breathed gently against me and watched me with one unblinking eye. He was as content in my hands as he would have been if he were lying on the riverbank in the sunshine, the gator wrestler told me later with a hint of awe in his voice. "You sure have a way with animals," he said. Maybe. Or maybe the gator just sensed that I wasn't aiming to wrestle him. Either way, I wasn't planning on making a pet out of any alligator—big or small—like the old-time settler did in the Fort Myers folktale about pirate treasure (*The Hermit*).

My final stop for the day was the airboat ride across the street from the museum. Stuffing cotton balls in my ears to help preserve my hearing against the loud engine, I laughed in delight as we swept out into the vast Everglades, zipping across the water and through the grass and scaring a blue heron, to visit a traditional Miccosukee village, carefully preserved on one of the  islands. We even made a side trip to see the ruins that were all that remained of the home of a traditional medicine man. I wondered if he had ever encountered black magic the way one medicine man had during the English settlement of Florida (*Little Lucy*).

It was with regret that I climbed back into the car and headed for the airport hotel where I would spend the last night of my research trip. It was a perfect end to a perfect trip, which had taken me from Jacksonville all the way down to Key West, zigzagging between the Atlantic and Gulf Coasts. During my time in Florida—once home to my grandfather Loyd—I met many wonderful folks, ranging from Conchs who'd lived in the Keys all their lives to immigrants newly arrived in Miami.

Florida is filled with people from all walks of life—farmers, businessmen, students, retirees, theme park managers, and artists. It was a privilege to meet them and hear their stories. And it was an honor to retell the wonderful folklore I collected from their beautiful state, which I first came to love as a child when staying with my grandfather. May you enjoy reading this collection of tales as much as I enjoyed writing it. And the next time you're in Islamorada, keep your eyes peeled around dawn—you just may see that ghost car I missed.

— *Sandy Schlosser*

PART ONE
Ghost Stories

1

The Antique Car

ISLAMORADA

I was up before dawn, pulling on my outdoor gear and grabbing my fishing poles out of the garage. I tiptoed so as not to wake the Missus, who had made it clear when we moved to Islamorada that retirement for her meant sleeping in every morning. When I asked her why she'd married a fisherman then, she threw a sofa pillow at me and laughed. But I knew she meant it, so I was always quiet when I left on an early-morning fishing trip.

Today I just wanted to throw my line in under the bridge and see what was biting. It was a pearly-gray morning with a soft mist curling around the edges of everything. The mist would burn off pretty quick in the light of the sun, but just now it made the world soft and mysterious. I paused to appreciate it for a moment, listening to the early morning grumbling of the gulls mixed with the call of a grackle. Then I put my gear into the car and backed out of the driveway.

A minute later I was pulling out on Highway 1, heading toward my favorite fishing spot. The mist was a little thicker inland, and practically no one was on the road. I kept up a steady pace for about a mile but slowed when I saw dim red taillights ahead of me. The mist was thinning now, and the pearly gray sky

2

was lightening with a bit of golden dawn as I hit the brakes and slowed down. In the uncertain light I saw a big old four-door antique car painted black in front of me. Its headlights were on, but they were much dimmer than mine. It was chugging along down Highway 1 as if it had all the time in the world to get where it was going.

Now I'm not an impatient man, but this car was going too slow for my liking. Still, what could I do? It was a double line right here, and it didn't look like the old behemoth in front of me had been the speediest of vehicles even when in its prime, which would have been circa 1930 if I judged it right.

I pulled my sedan closer to the car's back bumper hoping the chap inside would take a hint and head over to the side of the road so I could pass in safety. But he ignored me.

My headlights picked up the sandy color of his hair over the tall seat back. I wondered briefly who he was as I eased up on the accelerator and allowed more distance between our cars. I didn't know everyone in town, not by a long shot what with all the tourists that came here to fish. Still, I recognized most of the locals after living here a few years, and this fellow didn't look familiar. Course it was hard to tell from the back. Anyway, I didn't know of anyone hereabouts who owned an antique car like this one. Maybe he was an eccentric millionaire touring the Keys in a classic car, I mused as we put-putted along Highway 1.

We were the only cars on the highway at the moment. It was still too early for anyone but the most hard-nosed fishermen to be out. Well, and this crazy guy, I amended. Obviously he was awake too, though I didn't see any fishing gear sticking up out of his backseat. Could be in that big trunk, I speculated. It would be interesting to see where he turned off. Maybe we'd both end up fishing by the bridge.

We were nearing a bridge now, though not the one I aimed to fish. The big black car rumbled toward the bridge in the swirling mist, and for some reason my skin began to prickle as I followed it. The mist around the car was behaving strangely, blowing across the car instead of over it, as if it were being bandied about by a very strong wind. At the same time, I fancied I could hear wind howling all around me, though I felt nothing save the soft breath of the car heater. But in front of me, the antique car was shuddering as if pummeled by a gale I could not feel. It started up the slope of the bridge, swaying from side to side as if it were struggling to stay upright against a hurricane-force wind. Then the car tipped up alarmingly onto its side and vanished.

I gasped in alarm and hit the brakes. My sedan shuddered to a halt as I gazed in alarm at the now-empty road in front of me. What had happened? Had the car gone over the side of the bridge? I hadn't seen it fall over the bridge, and the guardrail was still intact. But I had to check. I pulled to the edge of the road, parked the car haphazardly, and ran onto the bridge.

As I reached the place where the antique car had disappeared, I walked into a cold spot and found myself standing in the darkest night, my body buffeted by a thunderous wind. I was immediately soaked by a painful tropical downpour. And right beside me I dimly perceived a large black car flipping over with a deadly bang in the force of that terrible wind. A second later I saw the black car slide off the side of the bridge, followed by a thunderous splashing that was so loud it could be heard over the monstrous storm. Just faintly above the crashing sounds, I thought I heard a man scream. Icy cold chills ran through my entire body at the sound.

Then I was catapulted back to the present by the loud beep of a car horn, followed by a familiar voice shouting, "Morning Jim! You're up early."

I blinked, and the golden light of dawn filled my vision. I was back on the bridge, and the mist was clearing under the first warm rays of the sun. I whirled around and saw that my next-door neighbor's car had slowed to a stop beside me. He'd rolled down the passenger window and was grinning through it. Then he saw the look on my face, and his grin vanished.

"Are you okay?" he asked in alarm. "I saw your car parked by the side of the road and figured you were looking for a place to fish. Did the car break down?"

I pulled myself together with an effort. My whole body was still shaking from the strange experience. Abruptly I jumped into the passenger seat and motioned my neighbor to pull over. He drove to the far side of the bridge and parked at the first turnoff.

"What happened?" he asked bluntly as I rubbed my chilled arms, trying to warm them as my mind replayed the scene over and over. Around us, the mist was lifting. The sun grew brighter as it rose, beaming golden rays over the lovely turquoise blue of the Atlantic Ocean.

Hesitantly, I told him about the antique car I'd seen, which had vanished on the bridge, and the cold spot I'd walked into just before he arrived in his car. Almost immediately he started nodding his head, as if he'd heard it before. I was relieved at his response. I figured he'd tell me I was crazy. Heck, I thought I *was* crazy. Cars—even antique cars—don't vanish into thin air. And that cold spot . . . Just thinking about it made shudders run up my spine.

THE ANTIQUE CAR

"You saw the ghost car," my neighbor said confidently. "It runs along the highway occasionally—mostly at night or in the early morning."

"A ghost car?" I asked in alarm.

"Yep," said my neighbor. "Been seen around here for decades. Folks reckon the car was blown off the bridge during the hurricane of '35. A lot of people were killed then, and the car looks like it was made sometime in the thirties."

I nodded in agreement. I'd heard quite a bit about the Labor Day Hurricane that had destroyed Flagler's railroad and much of the Keys. I was sure that more than one car had been blown off the road in that terrible storm. Anyway, it was as good an explanation as any, and it dovetailed nicely with what I'd heard and seen when I walked into the cold spot on the bridge.

My neighbor punched me lightly on the shoulder and asked, "Are you still up to some fishing? The Missus told me not to come home until lunchtime. She's working on a painting and doesn't want to be disturbed." (His wife was a retired artist who sold her work at one of the local galleries.)

"Sure," I said.

My neighbor turned his car around and drove me back to the place where I'd parked mine. Then we both drove to my favorite fishing spot and settled in for the morning. But as I tossed my line into the water, I decided that from now on I was going to drive the other way if I ever saw that antique car again. I'd had enough of ghosts!

2

Skyway

Dark clouds were rolling in fast from the Gulf as I made my way down the highway toward St. Petersburg in my eighteen-wheeler. I was making good time, so I kept up a steady pace and listened to NPR on the radio as heavy storm clouds moved across the sky, bringing an eerie green dusk with them. I caught a glimpse of lightning on the edge of the horizon and did a quick bit of calculating. If I kept up the speed I was going, chances were good that I'd hit the Sunshine Skyway Bridge around the same time as the storm. I didn't relish going across the fifteen-mile-long "engineering masterpiece" during a downpour, but luck wasn't with me. I kept rolling and so did the clouds, and we both were headed for the Skyway.

As the storm grew closer, the trees started bending in the gusty wind. It grew so dark I flipped on the lights. I could see the bridge ahead of me, and the sweep of my headlights caught something else. A blond figure in a white sweater was trudging heavily along the side of the road just ahead, approaching the bridge. My pulse gave a bang of alarm. The Sunshine Skyway Bridge, which crossed Tampa Bay, had had more than its share of suicides. The slumped shoulders and air of grief pouring off

8

the lone figure in front of me told me this might be another one if someone didn't do something.

Typical of our day and age, the cars ahead just rushed past without stopping. But I slowed down. My mama had raised me in the church, and I knew it would be on my heart for a long time if I didn't try to help that poor young girl trudging out onto the long Skyway Bridge just before a terrible thunderstorm.

I pulled alongside the blond girl just as a strobe of lightning lit the sky overhead. I rolled my window down and called to her, but my words were lost in the resulting clap of thunder. I had to repeat myself before the lonely figure—so wrapped up in grief she hadn't even noticed my truck pulling over—looked around and saw me.

"You look like you could use a lift," I said easily, giving her my best smile. "You don't want to be caught on the bridge in this storm."

Her face was pale and wan. There were lines of grief and pain around her eyes and lips, strange to see in one so young. She hesitated a moment, staring into my eyes. Chills ran up and down my arms at her look. There was something almost unearthly about it, as if—in her mind—she'd already crossed over to the other side. Then she gave me a very faint smile and nodded.

"Hop in," I said, as the first spatters of rain hit my windshield and a heavy gust of wind made the huge truck sway.

The girl bridged the few yards between us at a run as the heavens opened up. She jumped into the passenger's seat just as the rain began pouring down with its own kind of thunder.

"Make sure you buckle up," I said to my passenger as I put on the blinker and edged back onto the highway. She fumbled with the seat belt and then pulled it around her as the truck

SKYWAY

joined the other hearty souls crossing the Skyway during a torrential storm. The lightning display alone was worth the trip, though I didn't like the heavy gusting wind that made the truck jiggle and sway. It took all my experience as a trucker to keep us moving steadily as we crossed the long bridge.

"Where are you bound?" I asked the girl when I felt the truck was back under my control. I had to speak quite loudly to be heard over the rat-a-tat of the rain and the booming of the thunder.

The girl ducked her head so she could hide behind her long blond hair. "I don't really know," she muttered, so soft I could barely hear her over the rain. I caught a glimpse of tears on her pale cheeks just before a blond tress obscured her face. She started wringing her hands in her lap, and I figured I shouldn't push my luck. At least I'd gotten her into the truck, and unless she was truly suicidal, she probably wouldn't jump out while I was driving. At least I hoped not.

"This is some storm," I said lightly, gesturing briefly as a truly enormous sheet of lightning struck the opposite shore. It was followed by a clap of thunder that made my ears ring, and once again I fought for control as the wind gusted over the span of the bridge. We were climbing toward the peak now, and the wind was a bit worse up here.

Beside me, the girl straightened in alarm and clasped her hands in front of her face, as if in prayer. "Dear Jesus, forgive me!" she shouted suddenly. "Oh, forgive me!"

For a moment I thought she really would pull open the door and fling herself headlong out of the moving truck and over the side of the bridge. Instead she turned to face me, her blue eyes luminous in a face so pale that it seemed to glow with its own inner light. "Do you believe in God?" she asked in an intense voice.

11

And then she vanished from the passenger seat with a small puff of cold air.

I swore desperately and swerved a bit in my agitation—not a good move on a tall bridge in a thunderstorm. It took me nearly a minute to stabilize the truck, and I wasn't sure if the pounding fear in my head and heart was caused by the disappearing girl—let's face it, the disappearing ghost!—or by the possibility of driving the truck off the wet bridge and joining her.

I was still shaking when I reached the far end of the span, and I pulled off at the first exit advertising food. I drove around for a bit on the local roads, my body still trembling with shock and the profound, unearthly chill that filled the cab. Fortunately I found a local diner not too far from the exit and parked the truck at the back of the lot. I raced through the downpour to the nearest door. When I got inside, the server took one look at my pale face and trembling wet body and brought me a hot cup of coffee as soon as I sat down.

"On the house," she said as I took a grateful sip, spilling some of the hot liquid on my hands and shirt, since I couldn't keep the cup from trembling in my grip. She instantly grabbed napkins from the next table and watched as I wiped up the spill. I drank the whole cup down and half of another one before I calmed down enough to take in my surroundings. The dinner crowd hadn't arrived yet, so there were only a few patrons in the dining area and a couple of fishermen at the bar.

"Want to tell me about it?" asked the server as she handed me a menu.

I gulped a bit. "Is it that obvious?" I asked as I took it from her hand.

"I can tell you've had a shock of some kind," she said kindly.

I nodded and then told her my story. It took awhile. She sat down across from me with her pad and pen poised, as if she were about to take my order, so that the manager wouldn't yell if he saw her sitting there. And she listened with wide-eyed attention, as if she believed every word I said. It made me feel better.

"I've heard about that ghost," the server, whose nametag said AMANDA, said when I finished my story. "They say she was a local college student who committed suicide after breaking up with her boyfriend. That was a long time ago, I reckon. None of the cops who come in here have a record of a recent suicide matching her description. Still, you're not the only one to see her. It must have been really spooky."

"It was," I said, taking another sip from my second cup of coffee.

"Well, thanks for telling me about it," said Amanda, rising and waving her order pad at me. "You ready for something to eat?"

I nodded and ordered a hamburger "all the way," thinking that Amanda was very nice—and pretty too. I glanced at her hand as she headed toward the kitchen with my order. No wedding band. Nice.

I got Amanda's phone number before I headed out to my truck. She waved to me as I left and called, "Don't pick up any more hitchhikers."

"I won't," I called back, waving to her over my shoulder.

A practical, pretty girl like Amanda didn't come along every day, I mused. Not many girls would take a ghost story in their stride. She was pretty amazing. I decided that I wanted to take her out the next time I drove through St. Petersburg. And that's just what I did.

Many years have passed since that day. Amanda is still doing amazing things as my wife and the mother of our kids. And I'm still driving my truck. Amanda and I often joke about the fact that a ghost brought us together. But I haven't picked up any hitchhikers since that day.

3

In the Elevator

When my husband told me he'd booked a romantic weekend at the Biltmore Hotel to celebrate our fifth anniversary, I could hardly believe it. As the mother of twin toddlers, my days of romantic rendezvous and candlelight dinners seemed a world away from the daily grind of diapers and crying and cartoon characters on television. But it was true. Grandma was taking care of the little ones for a whole weekend, and we were getting away from it all.

The first thing I did was buy a stunning new dress of deep red with sequins that would make my husband's eyes pop. I'd worked hard to get my figure back after having twins, and this dress showed off how successful I'd been. Then I went hog wild and had my hair and nails done. For once, I felt like a beautiful woman and not just a hardworking mama. It was wonderful.

My husband picked me up after work on Friday, and we drove into Coral Gables and sheer luxury. I'd heard about the wonders of the Biltmore Hotel, but the reality was even more mind-boggling than the stories. There was the central tower, patterned after a tower in Seville, with the far-flung wings on either side. And my husband waxed eloquent over the golf courses as we drove up to the valet. After checking in, we went to peek at the huge swimming pool with its private cabana suites. Then my husband took me up to the luxury suite he'd booked in the tower. It was sweet!

"You're a princess for a day," he told me when I protested the expense. And it was true; I felt like a princess when I saw that suite. I flung myself gracefully onto the bed, rolled over, and started giggling like a little girl. My husband flung himself down beside me, and we laughed and cuddled and laughed some more. It was a flashback to our courting days, and I loved it!

We had dinner at the Fontana Restaurant, and I felt my whole body relax as we strolled the columned walkways and breathed in the perfumed night air. I wore the red dress, and it wasn't only my husband who gave me a second look that night.

"You're more beautiful now than you were in high school," my infatuated husband told me with a gleam in his eye. I gave him a sideways glance that promised a very happy evening ahead, and he squeezed my waist to seal the deal.

We wandered around the hotel after dinner, admiring the grand lobby with its pillared elegance, marbled floors, lofty painted ceilings, and carved woodwork before taking the elevator upstairs to our own piece of heaven.

My husband is crazy about golf, so he booked time with a pro the next morning while I went to the spa. We met for lunch and spent much of the afternoon by the pool in one of the private cabanas, lounging about and enjoying the peace and freedom. I finished the novel I was reading about 3:00 p.m. and rose luxuriously from my seat, saying, "I'm going to get another book. Do you need anything from the suite?"

My husband shook his head, not bothering to open his eyes. I smiled indulgently. He was almost asleep. I brushed a kiss against his cheek and then pulled a frilly feminine wrap over my bikini before donning sandals and heading inside. I pushed the elevator button and stood gazing happily at nothing, my head still back at the pool. I was the only one waiting for the elevator, but when the bell chimed and the door opened, I could have sworn that two of us got on. It was a strange feeling, and it disrupted my peaceful mood.

The door slid shut, the elevator started rising—and someone blew on my neck! I jumped and glanced around the luxurious interior. I was the only one inside the elevator. I could see my pale cheeks and startled expression in the mirrored wall. Just then, someone pinched my cheek. I felt it clearly. I gasped and backed up until I was pressed against the railing. What was going on?

I heard a distinctly masculine chuckle, right there beside me. At the same time, I realized the elevator had gone right past my floor without stopping. Frantically I jabbed the button, but the elevator kept going, only slowing when it passed the twelfth floor.

The elevator ground to a halt at the thirteenth floor, and I heard the bell chime. The doors opened in what I could only describe as a suggestive manner, and the smell of cigar smoke floated into the elevator. The whole atmosphere in the elevator was that of a man offering a romantic rendezvous to a pretty woman. Now I wasn't just frightened—I was offended.

"Just what kind of a girl do you think I am?" I said to the empty elevator doorway. "I happen to be very happily married!"

The elevator doors closed rather reluctantly, and the car started moving downward toward my floor. The invisible presence remained in the elevator with me, but he—it had to be a he!—seemed a bit subdued now. As the bell chimed at my floor and the doors slid open, I caught a glimpse of a corpulent

IN THE ELEVATOR

man leering at me from inside the mirror. He was staring suggestively at the frilly wrap that covered but did not obscure the pretty bikini I wore beneath. Completely freaked (and still offended), I glared at the man in the mirror, glanced around the empty (but for me) elevator, and sprang out the doors as soon as they opened. Someone slapped me on the derriere just before the elevator doors swished shut behind me. I ran all the way to my suite, and I took the stairs when I went back down to the pool.

I was still trembling—at least on the inside—two hours later when my husband and I rode the elevator upstairs to change for dinner. But no invisible man accompanied us on this trip, thank God. I hadn't told my husband about the incident in the elevator. He would have thought I was crazy. He didn't believe in ghosts or the supernatural and scoffed at such things. Still, I remembered hearing rumors that the Biltmore was haunted, so I paused to talk to a staff member after dinner while my husband was making another golf appointment for the next day. Hesitantly I told her what I'd experienced in the elevator, and she nodded at once in understanding. "That was Fatty," she told me. I blinked in surprise.

"Fatty?" I asked.

"Fatty Walsh, the gangster," she said. "He ran a speakeasy and high-stakes gambling casino on the thirteenth floor of the tower in the 1920s and early 1930s. He was shot and killed by a rival, but it was hushed up and the murder was never solved."

"Wow," I said. "And now he haunts the hotel?"

"Let's just say you're not the first woman to complain," the woman said with a grin. "Apparently Fatty was a womanizer, and he loved Cuban cigars."

Remembering the leering face in the mirror and the whiff of smoke I'd smelled on the thirteenth floor, I nodded. "That's him all right," I said.

"Well, look on the bright side," the woman said. "Fatty liked beautiful women. If he took the time to accost you, it means you've still got it!"

That made me laugh. "But do I dare tell my husband?" I asked with a chuckle.

"Tell me what?" asked my handsome husband, coming over to join our conversation.

"That your wife still has it!" the staff member said with a smile as I struck a pose in the shimmering red gown.

"You can say that again!" said my appreciative spouse, pulling me close for a kiss.

I thanked the woman, and we headed back upstairs to our romantic suite in the tower.

It was with great reluctance that we checked out of the hotel on Sunday morning and headed back to our suburban home. On the way, we chatted about the hotel and our favorite memories of the weekend just past. But there was one memory I wouldn't be sharing with my husband.

How do you tell a man who disbelieves in the supernatural that you've been slapped on the derriere by a womanizing ghost? I just couldn't do it. Maybe I'll tell him on our tenth anniversary!

4

Flight 401

THE EVERGLADES

We don't talk about Flight 401 much anymore. It was a tragedy, and our company was devastated by the loss of life that resulted from the equipment malfunction on that fateful December night in 1972.

The story begins a few months back, when one of our flight attendants started having dreams about a plane crash. In her repeated dreams, along with seeing flashes of Christmas trees and holly wreaths, she heard moans and screams and saw passengers fading away into dark waters. She became convinced that one of the company's planes would crash around Christmas, and she predicted that it would take place on a flight going to Miami.

Word spread among her friends within the company. Part of my responsibilities at the time included company morale, so I did my best to quash the rumors of an imminent disaster. But I was uneasy all the same and stayed alert during the holiday season, hoping the woman's predictions would be proved wrong. When Christmas Day passed without incident, I was relieved. Too soon, as it turned out.

The day of the crash, a last-minute roster change scheduled the psychic dreamer aboard Flight 401 for Miami, but she decided not to work that day and so was not aboard the plane when the equipment malfunctioned. The two pilots—both long-term pros—reported serious problems with the landing gear lights and the nose gear. Instructed by the tower to decrease their altitude and attempt a landing, the pilot brought the plane down to the requested altitude of two thousand feet and circled for final approach. Unknown to the flight crew, all the plane's instruments had already failed—they were flying blind. Instead of an altitude of two thousand feet, they were descending closer and closer to the waters of the Everglades, with no way of ascertaining whether the plane was level. As they made the second approach, a wing dipped into the water and the plane broke into several pieces, flinging passengers and crew like broken dolls all over the Everglades.

Rescue crews rushed to the area and pulled many of the injured from the dark waters and the wreckage, but in the end the final death toll stood at 101. It was a devastating loss that demoralized our company. The psychic flight attendant was hit particularly hard, as she was close friends with Captain Bob Loft and Don Repo, the pilot and second officer who were killed. Even her dreams hadn't been enough to save them.

Time moves on, of course. The survivors returned to their homes and their jobs. The dead were mourned and buried. The salvage crews pulled the remains of the plane from the Everglades, and the spare parts were recycled for use in other planes. Things gradually got back to normal for our airline.

Then, a few months after the accident, a friend who was a vice president with our company phoned me from Florida. I was surprised to get the call, since he was there on vacation. But my surprise gave way to shock when I heard what he had to say. He'd been flying first class—one of the perks of being an airline VP—and a pilot had taken the seat beside him. The VP thought he looked familiar, though he couldn't place him right away. He tried to strike up a conversation, but the pilot obviously didn't feel like talking. The pilot was pale and looked sad. The VP studied his face and felt a chill run over his skin as he suddenly recognized the man. It was Captain Bob Loft, who had died the night Flight 401 crashed into the Everglades. The eyes of the two men met briefly, and then the pilot vanished.

Hours after it took place, my friend was still shaken by the incident. I couldn't blame him. I felt shaky myself. A ghost! A ghost had appeared on one of our planes. It was hard to believe.

But this was only the beginning. Employees started seeing Captain Loft aboard other planes, and one crew reported receiving a safety lecture from the dead pilot. (I hope they listened!) Don Repo also began making appearances, sitting next to passengers and then vanishing into thin air. He too had the safety of our airline in mind and warned two flight attendants and an engineer that one of our planes would shortly have trouble with fire. He was right. On the return flight, the engine burst into flames in midair and had to be extinguished.

Well, this obviously wouldn't do. We couldn't have ghosts appearing willy-nilly on our planes, and I was asked to look into the matter. After investigating each of the alleged incidents, I began seeing a pattern. Many of the incidents took place on an L-1011, the same type of plane that went down in the Everglades during Flight 401—but not all of them. It wasn't until I started tracking the spare parts recycled from Flight 401

FLIGHT 401

that I hit pay dirt. Every ghostly appearance took place on a plane that was using one or more spare parts from the L-1011 jumbo jet that had gone down in the Everglades. At least now I knew the reason for the hauntings. And the solution was obvious: Remove the spare parts. I authorized the work at once.

That did the trick. The ghosts disappeared from our airplanes, and slowly the rumors died away, though the last reported sighting continued to linger in my mind. A flight captain on one of our Tri-Star jets saw the ghost of Don Repo on his flight. Reportedly the ghost told him that there would never be another crash on a Tri-Star jet. The ghosts would not let it happen. At the time, I was more pleased than not to hear those words. But things can have more than one meaning, as I realized when our company was forced to close its doors a few years later. No, we didn't have any more crashes on our Tri-Star jets—because we didn't have a company. It was ironic.

The last time I was in Miami, I had an airboat captain take me out to the place where Flight 401 went down. As is natural after a tragedy, all sorts of rumors had sprung up about this spot. People reported hearing screams and ghostly moans, seeing white faces beneath the dark waters of the Everglades, things of that ilk.

All I saw that fine, sunny day were egrets and blue herons. All I heard was the wind. It was a moment of great peace for me. I felt a burden I hadn't known I was shouldering fall from me. No matter what anyone else heard or saw in the future, my time among the phantoms of Flight 401 was complete. And I dared to hope that the phantoms would be at peace too. It was time to move on.

5

Old Red Eyes

Tilly was raised by an old aunt after her mother died and her father was sold to another master who lived far away from their plantation. Her aunt, descended from a long line of African princesses, was a conjure woman and healer who could summon the spirits—called Lords of the Manor—to her if she needed them.

Tilly and her aunt lived in one of the semicircle of houses made of tabby—oyster-shell cement. The semicircle was important, Tilly's old auntie explained to her. It was the pattern used by the villages back in Africa.

It was important to remember the old ways; to remember how they had lived when they were free and living back in Africa. Tilly had never been free. She had been born right on the plantation. But she still attended all the secret ceremonies held by her auntie and other folk who had come from their homeland, memorizing the ceremonies, learning some of the language. She was fiercely proud of her heritage, and fortunately their master was lenient about this sort of thing. He himself had married an African woman and set her free. Someday Tilly knew she would be free too. Someday.

In the meantime, she grew up tall and strong and very pretty. Her auntie was proud of her and started to teach her some conjuring. If she learned well, she might become the next conjure woman to support their slave village. Tilly wanted to learn, and she studied with a will.

Her studies were made all the easier by the master of the plantation, who used the "task" system to work his plantation. Under this system, a specific amount of work was required for each slave to finish daily. When the task was finished, the slave was free for the rest of the day. Tilly was very good in the household, and her auntie arranged for her to do the morning allotment of housecleaning, which left her afternoons and evenings free to tend their little garden, fix the meals, watch their chickens and other livestock, mend clothes, and study conjuring.

Life was pretty good, compared to what it might have been had they lived on a different plantation. Then one day the master brought home a new slave to work as a driver—what they called a supervisor on their plantation. Tilly hated the man on sight. He was big and broad, and some who didn't know better might have considered him handsome. But there was an evil red glint in his eyes that terrified Tilly, and she hated the way he undressed her with his eyes whenever they met. She always felt an ache in her mind—like the pain of a sore tooth—whenever he was near. Her old auntie took one look at the man and said that he had given his soul over to darkness. She forbade Tilly to have anything to do with him, and Tilly was happy to agree.

Fortunately her work at the house kept her away from the driver, whom she had secretly nicknamed Old Red Eyes. But the other ladies weren't so lucky. The woman assigned to work in the cotton fields or tend the indigo and other cash crops found themselves constantly under the eye of a cruel driver who both hated women and lusted after them. He was an excellent worker, and the master was pleased by the money rolling in. But fear was rising among his slaves, and Tilly's aunt grew more apprehensive each day, wondering how it would all end.

One afternoon Tilly finished her work early and headed back to the slave village, eager to complete the dress she was sewing as a surprise gift for her aunt. Two of their friends were marrying tomorrow, and she wanted her auntie to wear the new dress to the ceremony.

On her way home, she felt the familiar sore-tooth pain in her mind just before she saw the driver walking toward her down the main road. He was walking away from the slave village, which surprised her, since he was always out in the fields at this time of day. The driver's eyes scorched over Tilly as he approached, making her skin crawl. For some reason, the red glow within those dark eyes was very pronounced today. She nodded awkwardly to the driver and hurried past him, aware that he had stopped to watch her for a moment. An overwhelming sense of menace filled her. She swallowed hard against the lump in her throat, her back prickling as she felt Old Red Eyes's gaze upon her. She heard him take one step in her direction, two . . .

Then a shout of greeting broke the spell. Gib, the massive plantation blacksmith, was striding down the road, waving a lunch sack.

"Hello, Tilly. Done with your task already?" he called jovially.

Relief poured through Tilly. She felt her skin shuddering all over, as if she had just stepped into cool water. From the corner of her eye she saw Old Red Eyes whirl around and head back toward

the cotton fields as Gib stopped to pass the time of day with her. She felt, deep in her bones, that she had just had a narrow escape.

In her eagerness to complete the new dress before her auntie came home, Tilly forgot all about the unpleasant incident. When her auntie came through their door, the new dress was lying on the chair, neatly folded and tied with a white ribbon. Tilly's aunt exclaimed eagerly over her new gift and gave Tilly a huge hug, which made the young woman weep with joy. Their happy moment was interrupted suddenly by a scream from the other end of the slave village. Tilly and her auntie stared at each other in alarm before racing out of their small house to find out what was wrong.

A small crowd had gathered around a sobbing woman, who pointed with a shaking finger at the door of the brand-new house that had been erected for the newlyweds to move into tomorrow after their marriage ceremony. A few brave souls hurried inside to see what was wrong and hurried back out again at once, pale as ghosts, to be sick.

"What is it? What's wrong?" asked old auntie sternly.

They told her. It was murder.

Tilly gasped and hugged herself, unable to believe what was being said. Old auntie frowned grimly and walked into the small slave cabin, gesturing for Tilly to follow her. The stench hit Tilly before her eyes adjusted to the dim light inside—hot and earthy and metallic. Blood. It was blood. She blinked, willing her eyes to focus. She saw blood everywhere—on the walls, on the simple new furnishings made by the bride's father, and congealing on the floor.

The source of the blood was all too obvious. Three of her neighbors, young and beautiful slave women, lay violated and brutally slain upon the earth floor. They were heaped willy-nilly just inside the doorway, where anyone coming home from their daily task could see them. It was an act of mind-boggling disrespect and arrogance on the part of their killer. The familiar sore-tooth feeling that she associated with Old Red Eyes filled Tilly's mind, making her head throb with pain. And in her mind she again saw the driver—Old Red Eyes—hurrying away from the slave village in the middle of the day, when he had no business being there at all.

She closed her eyes for a moment, unwilling to see the familiar dead faces twisted in terror and fear. These were women she'd seen every day; women she respected and liked. It was too much. Her stomach was roiling, and she wanted to run away and be sick. But if she was going to be the new conjure woman, she had to face this. So Tilly opened her eyes and looked again at the gruesome scene, taking in every little detail. As she stared about, she could feel her old auntie beside her, quivering with suppressed rage.

When Tilly and her aunt withdrew from the violated house, they sent up to the plantation house for the master to come and see what had happened. While they waited for the master, Tilly told her old auntie what she had observed of Old Red Eyes on the main road. Old auntie nodded grimly. Her occult powers had told her who had done the deed immediately upon entering the new tabby house.

The master was swift to arrive—and even swifter to administer justice. The driver was strung up on an oak tree that grew next to the plantation's main road, and his body was buried in an unmarked grave. The newlyweds, quite naturally, did not want to live in the violated house, so it was torn down

and a new one was constructed on the other side of the village. The dead slave women were buried and mourned with proper respect. And life gradually resumed its normal pace.

About a month after the triple funeral, Tilly and her aunt were spending a peaceful evening in their small home, grinding herbs and mixing medicines at the table, when they heard footsteps pounding into the village. A moment later, someone began frantically knocking on their door and burst inside before they could answer it. Lily, one of the blacksmith's daughters, fell into their arms, gasping for breath, her eyes rolling in terror.

"Child, child, what is it?" cried old auntie as Tilly eased the girl into a chair.

"A ghost," the girl wailed. "A ghost assaulted me, auntie! Right out on the main road. A white mist came rising up from the old oak tree and became a man with glowing red eyes. I was so scared I couldn't move as he drifted toward me. Then he grabbed me with cold hands and pulled me right off the road toward the woods, whispering threats and tugging at my dress. I screamed and started shouting out all the holy prayers I know, which made him curse and release me. I ran for my life, and kept running until I got here!"

Tilly gasped and sat back on her heels. The old oak. It must have been the ghost of Old Red Eyes. The driver was still present, and he was still trying to hurt the innocent. Lily's sister had been one of his victims, and she was but one month buried under the cool earth. Tilly and her aunt exchanged a long look over the girl's head. This wasn't good. Not good at all.

Old auntie soothed the girl and sent her home with a mild sedative to drink at bedtime. Then she sat in front of the fire for a long time, not speaking a word to Tilly. She just hummed to herself and gazed into the flames, reaching out to the world around her with her supernatural senses. Tilly huddled in her chair and tried to do the same. She wasn't as good as auntie—not yet—but she did feel an ache in her mind, like an occult sore tooth, which might be the stirring of a cruel ghost.

Finally, auntie sighed and came out of her trance. "We're gonna have to go up to the oak tree tomorrow morning at sunrise," she said. Tilly nodded. Meanwhile, they both needed rest. It didn't do to mess with the occult when you were weary.

They were up long before sunrise, packing a bag full of conjure dust, herbs, and other tools of their trade. The walk to the hanging oak never felt so long to Tilly, and the sore-tooth ache inside her mind grew stronger and stronger with each step. Oh, yes. Old Red Eyes was back.

Old auntie stopped a hundred feet from the tree and quietly started the cleansing ceremony they'd discussed the night before. Yard by yard, they consecrated the whole area to the Lords of the Manor—those spirits who represented light and health and goodwill. It took nearly an hour. As they worked, the sore-tooth feeling faded a bit from Tilly's mind, but it did not go away completely. She mentioned this to her aunt as they walked home, as weary as if they'd done a day's task. Old auntie nodded grimly.

"Red Eyes is strong," she said. "A spirit like that won't just go away when we ask. But I don't think he will pull anyone else off the road after today's work."

Old auntie cast a sideways look at Tilly, and Tilly knew what was coming next. Old auntie wanted her to test it out. She wanted Tilly to walk past the old oak at dark that night and see if the spirit of Old Red Eyes attacked her. Tilly swallowed nervously at the thought. She knew old auntie would do it herself if her body wasn't so crippled with rheumatism that it made running impossible (should anything go wrong). *Please don't let anything go wrong,* the young conjure woman prayed to the Lords of the Manor. *Please.*

Tilly went out at dusk and sat quietly under a tree while a spectacular sunset colored the sky and then faded to the dark indigo of night. Slowly the stars came out, and still she sat, fingering the small pouch tied to her sash and meditating quietly. When everything grew quiet save for the wind in the palm trees and the small scampering sounds of night animals in the underbrush, Tilly rose. She patted the pouch again, rehearsing one last time the words and gestures she was supposed to use if the ghost arose beside her. Then she started toward the main road leading back toward the slave village.

Tilly walked slowly and purposefully, deliberately enjoying the balmy night air, the sparkle of the stars, the rustle of wings as a night bird took to the sky. And she made note of the moment when the sounds began to die away, as though every creature was hiding from something—or someone. The air became chilly, and gooseflesh arose on Tilly's bare arms. The wind picked up and blew along the road, whipping Tilly's long hair to and fro. There was a cold voice in the wind, and it was not a Lord of the Light that spoke.

The old oak tree was just ahead, a few yards from the main road. As Tilly neared the tree, a gossamer haze of white light appeared, hovering just above the ground. Tilly untied her sash with trembling fingers as the light grew larger and longer, twisting around itself in a spiraling motion that made the eyes ache. As she loosened the mouth of the pouch of herbs and conjure dust, Tilly saw the light form the silhouette of a tall man

OLD RED EYES

with glowing red eyes. She swallowed hard and took a steadying breath as the shadow-ghost, which was blacker than midnight save for a white glow outlining its edges and the bright red glow of its eyes, floated rapidly toward her. The sore-tooth ache was back in her head, throbbing hard. Tilly pushed at the pain until it settled into a spare corner of her brain, trying to free her mind to do her work.

Tilly waited until the shadow ghost reached the road. An arctic blast of cold air ran over her skin as Old Red Eyes reached its all-too-solid hands toward her. With a whispered prayer, Tilly threw a pinch of conjure dust into the ghost's face. The ghost flinched and ducked, raising a shadow hand to cover the glowing red eyes.

"Bone of my ancestors, push the ghost from this road," Tilly intoned. She sprinkled the dust on the road at her feet, and the shadow took a step back.

Tilly took a step forward, then another. "Dust of my ancestors, thrust the ghost from this road," she intoned, spreading another pinch of dust around her feet. The shadow gave a wail and fell back again, until its dark feet touched the grass on the side of the road.

Tilly moved forward, and the shadow moved with her, still desiring to possess her if it could. But each time it tried to step onto the road, small red sparks flew up from the dirt, pushing it back. The third time this happened, Tilly threw another pinch of dust at the shadow. Old Red Eyes wailed in fury, and the shadow-ghost lost its shape. All that remained in the roiling cloud of darkness was a pair of glowing red eyes.

"Spirit of my ancestors, keep the ghost from this road," Tilly intoned, sprinkling more dust at her feet. Carefully she went

35

through the gestures and words of the banishing ceremony they had used that morning, reinforcing them with the dust and herb mixture. With each word and gesture, the red eyes retreated back toward the tree, glaring malevolently at her.

When the last pinch of dust was gone, Tilly clapped her hands. A wall of light sprang up along the edges of the road. It acted as a barrier, prohibiting Old Red Eyes from stepping onto the road or dragging anyone off it. Beside the oak tree, the dark ghost gave a frustrated roar and disappeared with a popping sound like a cork coming out of a wine bottle.

Tilly sagged with relief. It was done. She said a final word of power, and the wall of light disappeared from physical view, though it remained there in the spiritual realm, holding Old Red Eyes back. It was the best she and old auntie could do. Old Red Eyes was beyond their power to banish, but at least they could contain him.

Tilly dragged herself home, too exhausted to do more than hand her old auntie the empty pouch and fall into bed. But old auntie knew the task was done. She'd felt it take.

From time to time, Old Red Eyes still appeared by the oak tree, especially if a pretty young woman went walking along the main road at night. But following the banishing ceremony, all that remained of the ghost was a glowing pair of malevolent red eyes that would follow the woman along the road for a few hundred yards, keeping pace with her no matter how fast she ran.

No one came to any harm from these encounters, but they were scary enough to make everyone in the slave village avoid the main road at night, which was probably just as well. Neither Tilly nor her old auntie knew what might happen if anyone stepped *off* the road near the old oak tree, and they didn't want to find out.

6

Diamond Ring

PENSACOLA

I paused for a moment to fluff my hair a bit before I swept up my long skirts with my hand and stepped out onto the crowded street. Everyone loved to stroll along Romano Street in the evening, and I was no exception. I loved to watch the crowds dressed in their finery, the young men and women flirting, the young ones racing about excitedly. I waved to everyone I saw, the diamond ring on my hand flashing in the light of the street lamps. For some reason, no one waved back, as if they didn't see me. It was a little odd, but I didn't let it bother me. I was out for a night on the town, and I looked my best. That was all that mattered.

At that moment, a handsome fellow who was obviously sparking a pretty girl looked up from his flirting and saw me strolling by. His mouth fell open, and his face paled a bit. I sometimes have that effect on men. His pretty girl poked him twice before he looked away, swallowing nervously. I tittered behind my lace handkerchief. Their reaction never grew stale.

Then the wind changed direction. It blew the smell of salt water. In an instant it all came back to me, as if it were only yesterday. The scene before me waivered. Suddenly the lights I saw came from old-fashioned oil lamps, and the people strolling the street were salty-looking sailors, men of business with their long-gowned wives, a few rough-hewn but kind-faced farmers, and of course me and my father, Don Irving Wharton.

We were laughing and talking with neighbors when we heard screams from the harbor. Everyone looked at one another in alarm, and my father thrust me behind him, reaching for his pistol. The screams grew louder, and suddenly a bunch of men burst onto the street, running for their lives. They were followed by a band of rowdy pirates, shouting curses, firing guns, and waving cutlasses.

"Pirates!" my father shouted. "Run, Sarah. Run!"

Men were already firing back at the invaders. Women screamed and ran into one another in their attempt to flee. Father fired, and one pirate went down. I stood behind him, frozen with fear.

"Run, Sarah," he screamed again as he desperately began to reload his pistol. At that moment, an evil-looking man with a long scar that bisected his face diagonally leapt upon my father from the shadows, knocking him over. I shouted in outrage and flung myself forward, beating at the man's back and sides with my tiny fists. He knocked me aside with one well-muscled arm, concentrating on my father, who was trying to rise. I fell backward and from my sprawled position saw the pirate raise his cutlass and thrust it through my father's heart.

I screamed again, fear and rage welling equally within me. Around me, pirates were overwhelming the townsfolk, and more than one woman was being ravished right on the street. Swearing that I would go down fighting, I leapt upon the pirate who had killed my father, knocking him off balance. I pounded both my fists on the back of his head, and he staggered under the assault. Behind us, I heard a man laugh. I was pulled off the murdering pirate by a huge, scruffy man who was better dressed than the others. I suspected it was the pirate captain. One look at his face told me what was in store for me.

"I like a gal with spirit," he said, flashing me a grin so that I could see his gold tooth.

I flailed wildly at the pirate captain, aiming for his eyes like my father had taught me. My self-defense training paid off. When my hand struck his eye, the diamond in my ring acted like a knife, smashing deep into the eye socket. To my complete astonishment, his eye popped out and rolled down his beard and onto the dusty ground. He gave a roar of pain and dropped me. I struck out at him again as I fell, and the diamond tore a piece out of his other eye.

He staggered around, blood pouring down his face. I scrambled back on all fours, trying to get to my feet, belatedly realizing that I should flee as my father had commanded. At that moment the pirate captain straightened up and, glaring at me through his one remaining eye, drew his cutlass so fast that I barely registered the movement. I backed up quick—until my back hit the wall of a building.

The pirate made one dramatic horizontal cut with the cutlass, decapitating me. For an instant, my body remained upright. Then it fell to the ground, leaving my spirit hovering above it, too stunned to do more than stare at my head as it rolled away. The diamond ring still sparkled on my hand in the lamplight.

The pirate captain staggered away, so bothered by his wounds that he forgot to rob me of my diamond. But the pirates around

DIAMOND RING

him were not so distracted, and all the jewelry was stripped from my headless corpse while my spirit hovered, helpless to stop them. I watched in shock while the pirates looted and burned the local buildings, killing the men and ravishing the women as they made their way through the town. The townsmen fought back and eventually drove the pirates off, but not before many lives were lost and much property was damaged or burned.

All this time, my spirit floated in a daze above my dead body. Finally neighbors claimed my body and that of my father. Not knowing what else to do, I followed them home. I watched as they helped my poor mother bury us. All the while, I waited for the light to come, for an angel to take me to heaven. But nothing happened. Once my body was under the ground, I started feeling very sleepy, so I closed my eyes.

When I opened them again, I was dressed in my blue frock with my hair done up all pretty and the diamond ring on my hand, standing on Romano Street. It was a beautiful night for a stroll, so I began walking along the street, calling greetings to the people I saw, though no one greeted me back, which I thought was strange. I couldn't understand why people didn't seem to see me.

Then the wind changed direction. It blew the smell of salt water into my face. In an instant it all came back to me as if it were only yesterday. The scene before me waivered. Suddenly the lights I saw came from old-fashioned oil lamps, and the people strolling the street were salty-looking sailors, men of business with their long-gowned wives, a few rough-hewn but kind-faced farmers, and of course, me and my father, Don Irving Wharton.

7

The Wedding

MAITLAND

When I read the wedding invitation, I was pleased to see that the ceremony was to take place in the chapel at the Maitland Art Center. I had heard quite a bit about the art center over the years. It was supposed to be absolutely gorgeous, the brainchild of artist Jules Andre Smith, who built the center on the shore of Lake Sybelia in the 1930s. Apparently the art center is one of the few surviving examples of Mayan Revival architecture in the Southeast. There are a number of structures within the center, linked together by beautiful gardens and courtyards.

"It has an Old World feeling," the bride-to-be told me when I phoned to RSVP the attendance of my husband and myself. "Come early so you have time to wander the grounds before the ceremony. You'll love it! Smith designed and carved quite a number of the embedded sculptures found throughout the grounds."

Just for fun, I read up on Jules Andre Smith before we went to the wedding. An American artist and architect who was born in Hong Kong in 1880, Smith earned a master's degree in architecture from Cornell University and was a self-taught etcher. During World War I, Smith commanded a group of eight artists, who were commissioned to sketch the American Expeditionary Forces in action on the front line. Those sketches were later housed in the Smithsonian Institution. Unfortunately, Smith's right leg was injured during training at Camp Plattsburg and had to be amputated after the war.

Even more tragic for an artist, Smith was forced to abandon his etching career in 1935 due to failing eyesight, although he was still able to publish a book of watercolors in 1836.

Smith later established the Maitland Research Studio in central Florida, where artists and sculptors were invited to come and create in an experimental fashion. A cement carving over the fireplace in the Center Gallery summarized the purpose of the center: "The artist's job is to explore, to announce new visions, and open new doors."

Smith died in 1959.

I studied a few of Smith's army etchings and found them haunting. I was quite eager to see the art center he had created.

My husband and I arrived an hour early and spent the time viewing the grounds and admiring the sculptures. The art center was just as lovely as anticipated, and a feeling of peace stole over me as I strolled around on my husband's arm. For some reason, I kept smelling cigar smoke as we ambled about, and I felt the uneasy sensation you get when someone is watching you. Once, I looked over my shoulder, as if expecting to see someone following us. But no one was there. I pushed the feeling away, determined to enjoy every moment of our visit to the art center. But I couldn't get the scent of cigar smoke out of my nostrils.

A few minutes before the ceremony, we entered the outdoor garden chapel that Smith had built in memory of his mother. An inscription at the entrance to the chapel said, "Let your thoughts

THE WEDDING

rest here awhile in beauty and in love." I pondered the words as we took our seats on the bride's side. The chapel only fit fifty seats, and they were nearly full when we arrived. We took a place near the back, and I stared around at the lovely decorations and sighed in delight when I observed the ornate cross carved into the back wall.

The music started, and the groom entered with his best man. And then the bride was walking down the aisle, absolutely glowing in her white dress and veil. She stepped up to her groom and took his hands, and I wiped a tear from my eye. Then I blinked in astonishment. Was it my imagination, or were there two brides at the front of the chapel? There was my friend, and there—behind the bridal party—was a figure in an old-fashioned bridal gown standing a little to one side of the minister who was officiating.

I was astonished. Who could it be? Then I realized I could—very faintly—see the wall of the chapel through the figure's body. At that moment, the figure vanished. I broke out in a cold sweat, goose bumps popping up all over my arms and legs. I wanted to run, but my whole body was frozen in place as the music swelled again and the brand-new husband and wife made their way triumphantly down the aisle.

My husband tapped my shoulder twice before I recovered enough to accompany him through the receiving line. The reception was set up in the Mayan Courtyard next door to the chapel, and all through the dinner, I mused upon what I had seen. Who was the ghost watching the ceremony so closely? Why was she—for I assumed from the gown that it must be a she—there? I had no answer.

One of the women at our table brought up the topic of Jules Andre Smith over dessert, and we chatted enthusiastically about the art center and about his watercolors and etchings. My new acquaintance mentioned casually that Smith had been obsessed with brides and had included one in several of his paintings. At her words, I broke into a cold sweat once again, remembering the figure I had seen. Did she have something to do with Smith?

There was dancing after the dessert, and my husband whirled me around the courtyard until my somber mood vanished in delighted laughter. As we approached the wall of the chapel, I caught another whiff of cigar smoke. Just for a moment I thought I saw the figure of a man leaning on a crutch, smoking contentedly in the corner. Then my husband twirled me around, and when I looked again, the man was gone. But his face haunted me. Where had I seen him before?

It wasn't until we bade the bride and groom farewell and headed toward the entrance that I realized, with a thump-thump of my pulse, that the man resembled the pictures I'd seen of Jules Andre Smith! And Smith had a wooden leg, which sometimes pained him enough to use a crutch. Could it be? *Not possible*, I told myself firmly. *You probably imagined him.*

And what about the figure in the bridal gown, a small voice whispered in my head as my husband opened the car door for me. "Double vision caused by tears," I said aloud. "It couldn't possibly be a ghost!"

"What did you say?" asked my husband, sliding into the driver's seat.

"Nothing," I said, absently looking back at the art center.

Was it haunted by the ghost of Jules Andre Smith? And who was the figure in the bridal gown? I shivered.

My husband turned the key in the ignition, put the car into drive, and took us home.

8

Shell Mound

CEDAR KEY

Charlie and I were boys together, getting into scrapes, driving our teachers crazy, and fishing—always fishing. Back in the 1940s, just about everyone in our town was employed as fishermen, and our families were no exception. Charlie's dad had a bad back and quit oystering about the time Charlie finished high school. So Charlie took over the business and asked me to join him. We made good money, being young and strong and willing to put in long hours. There was money enough for Charlie to buy a little house and propose to his high school sweetheart up on Shell Mound while sitting on a fallen log overlooking the estuary.

I was best man at Charlie's wedding, and a few years later he was best man at mine. I married a city girl who came to the Gulf Coast to visit distant relations and fell plumb in love with Florida, and with me. Esther took to fishing like she'd been born to it, and she was the one who suggested we do a little night fishing out near Shell Mound. Charlie's wife thought it was a great idea, and Charlie and I could fish anytime, day or night. So we loaded up the boat, packed a picnic, and set out for Shell Mound.

It was a wonderful night. The moon was full, and the tide was high. Moonlight shimmered upon the water, making a magic path that could lead to anywhere. I grinned a bit at my fancy and put my arm around Esther to protect her from the chilly wind that sprang up as Charlie navigated us toward one of our preferred fishing spots. We got our lines into the water and sat watching the dark shadow that was Shell Mound, not saying much, just enjoying the lovely night and the company of our best friends. My bride passed around cookies and lemonade, and we munched happily as I pulled in the first fish.

"Tell us a story, Charlie," his wife said lazily from her seat in the back of the boat. "Tell Esther the story about Shell Mound that you told me the day you proposed. We were sitting up there on a fallen log," she added to Esther, pointing toward the dark mound, which cast shadow over the water beneath it. "He dropped down on one knee and pulled out a little box with a diamond ring in it. Very romantic."

"That's me. Very romantic," said Charlie, tossing a crab into a bucket at his feet.

I felt another tug on my line and started reeling in as Charlie told Esther the ghost story local folks had been talking about for decades.

"Back in the 1800s, pirates still roamed Florida's Gulf Coast," Charlie began as he baited another crab trap and lowered it into the water. "It was a dangerous time. Pirates knew no mercy when it came to pillaging, plundering, and protecting their treasure. And some of them had real treasure to protect."

According to Charlie's story, one not-so-merry band of pirates had accumulated a large chest of treasure and were looking for someplace to stash it, since the authorities were hot on their heels. One of the men had heard about Shell Mound and thought it would make a good hiding place. So the pirates rowed up to the key late one moonless night with the treasure chest and carried it up onto the mound.

They were busy digging a deep hole to hide their treasure in when a local girl named Annie came walking around Shell Mound with her dog at her heels. No one knows for sure what brought Annie out that night: a rendezvous with her beau, a need for some fresh air, or maybe she was meeting some friends to do some night fishing, like we were tonight. Whatever the reason, it was her misfortune to come upon a band of ruthless pirates burying treasure, and it cost Annie her life. She was shot where she stood, frozen in surprise and fear. Her dog went ballistic, and he was shot too. The pirates lowered the treasure chest into the hole and threw Annie and her dog on top of it. Then they filled in the hole and covered it with grass, shells, rocks, and other debris to camouflage the place before they rowed back to their ship and sailed away.

Annie's folks didn't know what had become of her. They looked everywhere, and some ugly rumors got started saying that she'd run away because she found out she was in the family way.

The truth wasn't discovered until three months later, when Annie's pa was out fishing near Shell Mound and saw the ghost of his daughter walking near the foot of the mound with her dog at her heels, just as she had done in life. After a moment of shock, he spoke to his daughter, and she answered him in an eerie voice that rang softly like bells and brought goose bumps up on his flesh. She told him about the pirates and their treasure, adding a warning at the end of her tale. The pirates had filled the hole with quicklime before filling it in. Only a person with no greed in their heart could dig up the treasure.

"Course Annie's parents went searching for their daughter's body—and the treasure," Charlie concluded. "But they didn't find it. No one did, not in all the years it's lain there. Some folks think the pirates returned and took it away with them. Some say its still there, waiting for someone without any greed in their heart to claim it. And Annie's ghost is still seen from time to time, walking on or near Shell Mound with her dog at her heels."

"Spooky," Esther said with a shiver. "And I was just going to ask you to pull up on shore so I could take a nature break. Now I'm not so sure!"

"I need to go too," said Charlie's wife. "We can protect each other from the ghost."

Esther chuckled a little nervously and agreed. Amiably, we pulled in our lines and rowed ashore. I helped the ladies out and sat aboard with Charlie, listening to an owl hooting and the lap of the water against the shore.

The girls were taking a rather long time about their business, as girls often do, and I was getting a might restless when a bright light suddenly shone in the woods behind me. I whipped around in time to hear Esther scream. Alarmed, I jumped out of the boat and ran forward, Charlie at my heels. And then we saw the girls running toward us in the moonlight. Behind them floated the glowing figure of a woman with long dark hair, a light-colored blouse, and an ankle-length dark skirt. Her face was just a blur of white light, but the little dog trotting at her side a few inches above the ground was as clear as day. I leapt forward, whirled Esther up into my arms, and ran for the boat.

Charlie and his wife were right behind us. Charlie dumped his bride unceremoniously into the bow and pushed off. Esther and I clung together in the stern, watching in awe and terror as the ghost continued her leisurely walk around the side of the mound and vanished into the woods.

"I want to go home," Esther said in a shaky voice. "I want to go home right now."

"Me too," Charlie's wife added through chattering teeth.

I couldn't blame them. My heart was pounding against my ribs, and funny chills were running all over my skin like little spiders. I shuddered and started the motor, and we headed back toward civilization in silence. Esther wrapped herself in a blanket and tucked herself under my free arm. Charlie and his wife were huddled together under the other blanket, speechless with the shock of what we had seen.

When Shell Mound was out of sight, Esther relaxed a little. I asked her what had happened.

"We were . . . um . . . using a handy tree as a ladies room when a bright light suddenly appeared on the path," Esther said. "We . . . uh . . . pulled ourselves together real quick, not wanting to appear in a disheveled state before strangers. Then we stepped out onto the path and saw the ghost-woman floating toward us. She was real pale, and we could see the trees right through her body! I guess we panicked then. I know I did. I screamed and ran down the path as fast as I could go. And then you were there and we were in the boat, and well . . . you know the rest."

I certainly did. It was a dramatic end to our night-fishing adventure, and we were all rather subdued when we docked the boat and went to our separate homes. But thinking back on it as I readied for bed, I was glad I'd gotten a glimpse of our local

SHELL MOUND

legend. It would be a story to tell my grandchildren. When I said as much to Esther, she agreed with me.

"But," she added, having the last word as usual, "I think we should choose another spot for night fishing from now on. One ghost sighting is enough for this lady!"

And I had to agree.

9

Ghost Baby

ORLANDO

She hated walking home past the cemetery at night, but their family was too poor to own a car since their father had lost his job in the financial crash of 1929. The Great Depression, they were calling it, and to her the term "depression" had a double meaning. It was how she felt when she realized she had to drop out of school and get a job—any job—to help put food on the table for her large family. She hated giving up her dream of going to college and studying to be a nurse, but she was the eldest, and her mother was an invalid and too weak to hold down a regular job. So she got work waiting tables at a local restaurant, and every evening she walked home past the cemetery.

It was an old cemetery and very creepy, with looming tombstones—many old and broken—strange statutes, and carvings on the headstones. Dark shadows seemed to follow her as she walked past each evening. There was one particular statue of an angel that watched her wherever she went with blank eyes that still seemed to register her every move. It made her skin crawl every time she saw it. She had always thought angels were beautiful, but in her mind this angel statue represented Death, and she hated it more passionately than she had ever hated anything in her life. The cemetery had come to typify everything that was currently wrong with her life.

She tried to work the day shift so that she need not pass the cemetery at night. But when one of her fellow waitresses got sick, she was forced to do double duty at the restaurant—and walk home past the cemetery after dark. For the first week, she managed to find someone walking her way each night so that she had company when she hurried past the graveyard. But ten days after her shift change, no one she knew was heading that way. Still, she told herself, it was early enough for businessmen and women to still be walking the streets. Someone would be there when she arrived.

As she turned into the street where the cemetery lay, she realized with a painful thudding of her heart that she had been wrong. There was no one else walking there that night. The street was deserted. And aside from the pools of light cast by a couple of streetlamps, it was quite dark. She stopped at the crosswalk, frozen with dread. She could see the line of tombstones, the looming statues. And halfway down the street she could dimly make out the figure of the angel, the Angel of Death.

She swallowed against bile that rose at the back of her throat. She couldn't walk down that empty street. She couldn't. Shudders of terror ran through her thin frame, and she clutched her coat against her body with shaking hands. A cold breeze swirled down the road and bit right through her. In the pool of light underneath one of the streetlamps, she saw the white petals of a flower whirling in a tight circle, as if they had been picked up by a whirligig. It was all that remained of a funeral lily.

At the sight of the floating petals, she leapt back around the corner and stood with her back pressed against a building, heart pounding in terror. She would go back to the restaurant where it was warm and light. Perhaps she could phone the neighbors, since their own phone had been shut off when they couldn't pay the bill. One of the neighbors would surely run across the street and ask her father to come walk her home. She drew a shuddering breath and sighed in relief at this plan.

And then she heard it: the wailing cry of a baby. The sound was coming from the cemetery. She froze, goose bumps crawling up her arms to her shoulders, the hairs on her neck standing on end. What was a baby doing in a cemetery on a chilly winter night? But she already knew the answer to that, and her feet, unbidden, were already turning the corner and walking down the empty street toward the cemetery. More than one infant had been abandoned by its parents since the Great Depression hit. Maybe they couldn't afford to feed it, or perhaps it was born out of wedlock. The cemetery was as good a place as any to drop an unwanted infant. All the compassion within her—the compassion that made her yearn to be a nurse—was aroused by baby's cries. She would rescue it and take it to the nearest hospital. She couldn't just walk away, no matter how creepy she found the cemetery at night.

She searched the shadows for the source of the noise, bent forward against the strong, cold wind that whistled down the street. In the light of the second streetlamp, she saw a bundle lying on a raised tomb. It was not just any tomb. No, it was the tomb that had the statue of the Angel of Death looming over it.

She gulped, her knees weakening so that she staggered and fell against the lamppost. She couldn't do it. She couldn't walk up to that tomb, right under that angel. But she had to. The baby gave a lusty cry, and the sound pierced her heart. She pushed

away from the lamppost and hurried through the gate into the cemetery. She kept her eyes fixed on the squirming bundle lying on the lid of the tomb, trying to ignore that statue of the angel, which followed her with its eyes. She snatched up the baby and cradled it in her arms, gazing down into its chubby round face. Its blue eyes were full of tears as it looked up at her. It gave one last little whimper and then stopped crying.

"Hush little one," she whispered. "You're safe now."

The baby weighed hardly anything at all, she marveled, turning quickly away from the flickering dark shadows beneath the angel. She hurried toward the gate, anxious to leave this horrible place. With each step, the baby in her arms weighed a bit more, until her arms felt leaden and she was afraid she would drop it. She staggered, slowing with each step, and glanced down again at the infant. The face she saw made her gasp in horror. It was the twisted, leering face of an old man. Scraggly white hair sprang all over its head, writhing as if it were alive. It grinned at her through withered lips, baring sharp fangs. And one tiny, clawed hand flashed upward and raked across her cheek.

She screamed in pain and horror, throwing the terrible imp away from her. The bundle hit the ground with a thud, and red smoke began billowing out of the blankets. She screamed again and ran for her life, pursued by a flaming cloud of smoke that smelled of brimstone and ashes. The flaming form had taken on the figure of a tiny, demonic man.

She leapt through the cemetery gates, and the flaming figure bounced off the empty space between the gates as if it were an invisible wall. Instantly it vanished and she fell against the lamppost, shaking with sobs, her legs trembling too much to hold her upright.

GHOST BABY

The whole world had gone silent save for the heavy gusting of the breeze. A few flower petals flew out of the cemetery and whirled around the lamppost. And into the silence came the wail of a baby. Glancing involuntarily toward the cemetery, she saw the bundle reappear on top of the flat tombstone.

All the strength returned to her legs in a flash, and she ran down the haunted street and all the way home. She raced through the kitchen door and slammed it shut behind her. Her mother took one look at her bleeding cheek and hurried over, exclaiming in horror. Her whole family gathered around the table as her mother cleaned the three claw marks on her right cheek with antiseptic and carefully bandaged the wound.

"A ghost baby," her father said, holding tightly to her hand. "That was a ghost baby you saw in that cemetery. I'm sorry, honey. If I'd known such a thing was haunting that cemetery, I'd never have let you walk home alone."

"What's a ghost baby?" her younger brother asked as she buried her head against her father's shoulder and wept unashamedly.

"I don't rightly know, son," her father replied. "Some folks say it's the spirit of an infant that died before its time. Others say it's a demon from hell, come to lure unwary victims into its lair to kill them."

"Oh," gasped her wide-eyed brother. "I think you had a close escape," he said to his weeping sister.

"I think so too," she said, straightening up and wiping her eyes. "I don't ever want to walk down that road again, Papa," she added.

"You're not going to," her father said firmly. "I'll talk to the neighbors tomorrow. I'm sure they will drive you to work and back if your mama will babysit for them once a week."

"You think they will?" she asked hopefully.

"I know they will," her father said firmly.

And they did. For the next two years, her neighbor's handsome son drove her to work each morning and picked her up from work at the end of her shift. And when her father got a new job and she was able to go to college, her neighbor's son drove her to college too. They married a month after she graduated, and she went to work as a nurse when they got back from their honeymoon. So the ghost baby did her a good turn after all. But she never went near that cemetery again.

10

The Phantom Coach

TALLAHASSEE

Judd was over the moon the day he learned that Tess loved him—absolutely over the moon. She was the prettiest girl on the whole plantation. She could take her pick from any of the men who flocked to her door, and she had chosen him! It was amazing! Every chance he got, Judd would pick wildflowers for her, dance with her under the palm trees, sing love songs to her. She'd giggle and preen and call him "honey." He melted like ice cream in the hot sun when she called him "honey."

They planned to be married in June, and Tess was sewing every moment she could spare from her house duties, making a wedding quilt and other items they needed for their new home. And when he wasn't bone weary from working in the fields, Judd was building them a small cabin of their very own with the help of his friends. It was a wonderful time full of love and courtship.

About a month before the wedding, a couple of Judd's friends suggested they throw a big jamboree on Saturday night when they were done working in the fields. It sounded like fun, so they passed the word around the cotton fields, and someone ran the news up to folks working in the big plantation house.

Everyone was real excited about the party, and they discussed it all week. On Saturday night, the girls hurried to their cabins to dress in whatever finery they had, while the fellows washed up and then came to escort their ladies to the jamboree. With Tess on his arm, Judd knew he was the envy of everyone as they walked toward the big open space at the center of the plantation for the dance.

One of the lads had his fiddle and another had a drum. Someone showed up with a recorder, and other instruments were produced. Within moments, the impromptu band was hauling and scraping away at a favorite tune, and Judd whirled Tess into the crowd to dance. The moon was full, and the smells of stew and dumplings and other good food came from the tables where the older ladies were chatting as they set up for dinner. Someone had put a barrel of moonshine on a large stump next to the tables. Oh, my, he was happier than he'd ever been in his life.

The jamboree was in full swing when they heard the jingle of a harness and the sound of horses' hooves coming along the lane. The musicians faltered, and everyone stopped dancing. As the music died, folks around the eating tables turned to see what was wrong. Everyone watched as the carriage lanterns drew closer and closer, revealing a team of horses pulling the Master's carriage driving up the lane toward the jamboree. By the time the Master halted his horses, there was complete silence in the meadow.

"I've come to the jamboree," the Master announced, swinging down from his phaeton and throwing the reins to a man standing near by. "Please, don't stop dancing on my account!"

He waved imperiously to the musicians, who glanced uneasily at one another and then resumed the tune interrupted by the Master's arrival. Slowly folks returned to the impromptu dance floor, and the Master clapped his hands and nodded in approval. One of the housemaids brought him a mug full of moonshine, which he downed in one gulp.

After a few moments, everyone began to relax, but the jamboree did not return to its former exuberance. Everyone was too conscious of the Master to let go and truly enjoy themselves. Judd and Tess stopped dancing and went over to get some stew, steering clear of the Master, who sometimes pestered the beautiful Tess when she served in the house. But the Master was not to be avoided. He was already on his fourth glass of moonshine, and when he saw Tess across the table from him, his eyes began to gleam. Tess hastily put down her glass and grabbed Judd urgently by the arm, whispering: "Quick, let's dance."

Before he could lead her to the dance floor, the Master was looming in front of them. The Master pushed Judd aside, grabbed Tess around the waist, and caressed her inappropriately. Judd's eyes bulged at the sheer audacity of the man. Anger roared through his gut. Tess was his girl. They would be married in June. How dare he? How dare he!

Judd barged forward, yanking Tess out of the Master's arms and throwing the Master back against the tables. The Master landed in the stew pot, and the table broke under the impact, throwing the Master to the ground and covering him in soggy dumplings.

For a moment, the Master gaped at Judd, his mouth wide open with shock. Then the Master leapt up with a drunken roar and dove headfirst into Judd's stomach. The fight was on then. Several men tried to pull them apart, but Judd had a lock on the Master's head and wouldn't let go. The Master was pummeling him left-right, left-right in the ribs, which made it hard to breathe. Then the Master slid down unexpectedly, throwing Judd off balance, and he tumbled right over the Master's head and landed on the ground. The Master was on top of him at once, and they rolled back and forth, first one and then the other gaining the upper hand. The rolling took them onto stony ground, just as Judd slammed a left hook against the Master's jaw. The Master's head jerked back and struck a stone underneath him. The Master froze and all expression drained from his face. He went very still.

Judd gasped and sat back on his knees, unsure of what had just happened but feeling a sinking sensation deep in his gut. Two men dragged him off the Master and then reached down to help the Master up. They froze in much the manner of the Master a moment ago. Judd knew by the look on their faces that the Master was dead, but he did not know how or why. His final blow hadn't been hard enough to kill the man.

When they moved the Master at last, Judd saw the answer. A sliver of rock about five inches long and sharp as a stiletto knife had pierced through the Master's skull when his head whipped backward from the punch. The men had to tug at the Master's hair to lift his head off the knifelike stone. To Judd's amazement, the wound bled very little and seemed to disappear beneath the Master's hair, leaving just the smallest trace of blood on the sharp sliver.

At that moment, Tess raced to Judd's side and grabbed hold of his arm. One look at the Master's limp body told her what had happened. Fiercely, she whispered to the men standing over the Master's body: "Judd was defending my honor! It was self-defense."

One of the men grouped around the dead Master was Tess's father. He looked at his daughter, looked at Judd, and then shouted to the crowd, "The Master's just stunned. And drunk. Let's get him into the carriage and take him home!"

Tess's father nodded to the other fellows in the group. Together they lifted the Master and "walked" him to the phaeton, keeping their bodies between the crowd and the Master and sticking to the darkest places in the meadow.

Within minutes, the phaeton drove back up the lane with the Master in the front passenger seat and Tess's father and Judd in the driver's seat.

"This never happened," Tess's father said quietly as they got down from the carriage, leaving the dead Master in front of the mansion. "The Master died during the ride home from a heart attack or something. The family will find his body in the morning."

Judd nodded uncertainly. "Will someone tell the authorities about the fight?" he asked as they started walking back toward the jamboree, which had picked up in enthusiasm and volume with the departure of the Master.

"No one will tell," Tess's father said firmly. He was the unofficial headman of their slave village and the foreman over the cotton fields. His word was law among the slaves on the plantation. No one would tell.

To Judd's surprise, the doctor ruled the death a heart attack, and the Master was buried with all the pomp due his elevated station in life. The son took over the plantation, and life resumed a normal pattern.

Judd had tried to break things off with Tess, not wanting her to marry a marked man. But Tess insisted they go through with the wedding. Eight weeks after the jamboree, they were living in their new cabin and sleeping under the wedding quilt she'd stitched so diligently.

Two days after the wedding, Judd was kept late in the cotton fields and was walking home in darkness when he heard the familiar rattle of a carriage coming up the lane. The moon was full, and he saw the light from the carriage lantern swinging back and forth with the motion of the horses. But, he realized suddenly, there were no horses pulling this carriage! There was just an empty harness jingling and tugging as actively as if there were invisible horses within it. And looming in the driver's seat of the black phaeton was the pale, glowing figure of the old Master, his withering face empty of expression, just as it had been when he was impaled by the sharp stone. The phantom's blue eyes were opened, and they were fixed blankly upon his killer. There was no malice on the face. It was just blank and dead looking, which somehow made it even more ghastly.

Judd's body trembled cravenly at the sight of the Master. His throat tensed so hard it choked him, and his breath came in great gasps. Just when he thought he was free and clear, the dead Master had risen again!

Suddenly the carriage swerved and the Master and his invisible team barreled full speed toward Judd. He gave a mighty scream and ran for his life, the invisible horses on his heels. Judd fled down the dark lane and raced right through the slave village with the phantom carriage behind him. Every family came running to their door to see what the fuss was about, and everyone screamed in panic when they saw the dead Master chasing Judd through the village.

Judd heard Tess shouting his name, but he didn't even slow down. He raced past the last house and dived into a narrow gap between the trees, hoping the phantom carriage could not follow him yonder. But the dead Master and his invisible horses rushed onward, moving effortlessly through the broad trunks of trees and impenetrable vines and bracken, while Judd stumbled and cursed and got caught on branches and tangled up in briars. By the time he burst out onto the lawn of the mansion, he was a sight—tattered clothing, bleeding from multiple scrapes, bruised in every limb. And the phantom carriage remained at his heels.

Just when Judd thought his lungs would burst right out of his chest and his heart shatter into a million pieces from sheer fright, the carriage reached the driveway in front of the manor house. It pulled up to the front door . . . and vanished in the exact spot where Judd had left it eight weeks ago.

Judd fell onto the grass, panting desperately as he gazed up at the full moon. Lord, that was close! He knew one thing for certain. He wasn't staying another minute on this haunted plantation. Better to risk the uncertainties of a runaway slave than certain-death by ghost. One more encounter of this kind would kill him, sure enough.

As soon as his legs would hold him, Judd walked back to his house, packed a bag, and headed north for Canada. Tess went with him. There was a hue and cry when the two slaves were discovered missing, but no one in the slave village blamed them for running. And fear must have leant Judd extra cunning, for they were never caught.

THE PHANTOMCOACH

Folks hereabouts reckon Judd did the right thing, because the phantom carriage showed up again next month during the night of the full moon, with the old Master in the driver's seat urging invisible horses up the lane to the mansion.

There's only a ruin now where the old plantation house once stood in magnificence. But each month on the night of the full moon, the phantom carriage still makes its way through the tangled overgrowth toward the place where the old Master's body was dumped so long ago.

11

The Cypress Tree

We were cutting lumber along the Escambia River that year of 1929, and we were making some good money doing it. That was good, because work was scarce in other parts of the country, and folks couldn't feed their loved ones. The crew was a rough bunch of lumberjacks, but they were goodhearted and a bit superstitious, as all lumberjacks are. So when we reached a certain stretch of the river, I wasn't surprised to hear my men talking about the ghost.

"There's a ghost on the river?" asked one of the new fellows over dinner. He was a city slicker who'd just moved to Florida from New York and decided to try the life of a woodsman. The other lumberjacks enjoyed pulling his leg, and Hank was the best at it. Hank put his fork and knife down on his plate and asked, "You ain't heard the story about the armored Spaniard?"

The city slicker stared at him, wide eyed as a little kid. He shook his head, and Hank grinned slyly and told him the story of the Spaniard.

A long time ago, back when the Spanish ruled Florida, a young soldier named Juan Alverado was assigned to a unit in the Escambia region. Alverado wasn't happy with the assignment.

He'd been working in Cuba and had himself a pretty sweetheart there. But he obeyed his officers and boarded a ship for Florida.

Alverado's first task was to accompany a party of explorers upriver. The explorers were mapping the region with an eye to building a new road along the river. No easy task to be sure as the area was dangerous enough that they had been granted a group of soldiers to guard them. In addition to Alverado and his fellow soldiers, the explorers also hired a couple of native tribesmen to guide them along the trail. And that's where the trouble started.

A few weeks into the journey, Alverado and another soldier accompanied the tribesmen on a foraging and hunting mission along the banks of the river, looking for meat and fruit to supplement their rations. Alverado's buddy started harassing one of the tribesmen—or perhaps it was the other way around. Alverado never really knew what started it. But suddenly the tribesmen were attacking the soldiers and Alverado was fighting for his life. The other soldier was killed in the confrontation, and Alverado was wounded. Alverado managed to stab his knife into the calf of one of the tribesmen, bringing the man down. Then he fled, stumbling and bleeding through the unfamiliar woods with the tribesmen in hot pursuit. According to the locals who heard the tale from the tribesmen involved in the skirmish, Alverado managed to elude his attackers and escape with his life. But he never made it back to the exploration party, and the Spaniards assumed that he had deserted the army and returned to Cuba and the arms of his sweetheart.

After a few months, tribesmen in the area started seeing an apparition along the banks of the Escambia River. A Spanish soldier would appear on the banks at sunset, deathly pale and

THE CYPRESS TREE

glowing softly in the deepening twilight. He would wander aimlessly for a few minutes and then vanish.

"Everyone assumed the Spanish soldier who had died during the skirmish was haunting the riverbank," Hank said. "Although *I* think it is the spirit of Alverado. After all, he was never seen again after that day. The Spaniards assumed he'd deserted, but he may have died alone in the woods. That would be enough to turn any man into a ghost, to my mind."

The city slicker was so engrossed in the tale that he'd forgotten to chew. It was only after Hank concluded his tale that he swallowed his bite of pancake and asked, "Is that where we are going to log tomorrow? That part of the Escambia?"

"That's where we're going," Hank said with an evil grin. "You let me know if you see the ghost. If you do, ask him which one he is, Alverado or the other soldier!"

Chuckling to himself, Hank rose, stretched, and went to get some shut-eye. The rest of us followed. But I don't reckon the city slicker slept well that night.

The following day had us lumbering along the river. I didn't believe in ghosts myself, so it was business as usual for me. I could tell some of the men were nervous, though, until I gave them a sharp talking-to about keeping their mind on their work. Hank just took another draft of his cigarette and grinned. I motioned for him to help the city slicker, and together they tackled a massive cypress tree growing near the banks of the river.

They were about halfway through their cut when the tree made a terrible groaning sound like that of a dying man and split in half. Everyone looked around at the sound, and then Hank leapt backward and gave a startled shout. We dropped everything and ran to see what was what. The city slicker had climbed halfway up a nearby sapling in his fright and was trembling like a baby. Hank was staring into a huge hollow pocket inside the tree. Inside the hollow was a skeleton dressed in Spanish armor.

"B . . . boss," Hank said, his normally cheerful voice rather shaky. "I think we just found Alverado."

I stared in amazement at the corpse, fear inching up my arms and raising tiny hairs all over my body. "I think you're right," I said, managing to sound casual and cool in spite of the terror wrenching at my middle.

"He must have crawled into that hollow to hide from the Indians," the city slicker babbled, sliding down from the sapling as he stared bug-eyed at the skeleton, "and died from his wounds before he could get out."

"And the tree grew right over him," Hank finished the story, grinding his cigarette out on a fallen log with trembling fingers.

We all nodded soberly. There was no other explanation for it. To ease the fears of the men, I said a prayer over the dead Spaniard before we pulled his body out of the tree. We took it back to Pensacola and turned it over to the authorities. They gave Alverado a proper burial in the local cemetery, and after that, the ghost sightings on the bank of the river ceased.

So Hank was right. The ghost *was* Alverado, trying to lead folks to his corpse. He wasn't a deserter after all.

12

Dark Dreams

MIAMI

Elena was sitting at the kitchen table with her mother, planning the menu for her engagement party, when her father walked in and told them to pack immediately. Elena and her mother looked up in alarm. It was early 1959, just a few days after the new government had taken over Cuba, and they were all feeling nervous about what the future held for them.

"What do you mean, pack?" Elena exclaimed.

"We are going to your uncle in Miami," her father said, exchanging a serious look with her mother. "Tonight."

"Is Uncle Juan ill?" Elena asked. Uncle Juan was her favorite relative.

"Pack, Elena," her father said, pointing to the stairs.

Caught up in the urgency of his manner, Elena hurried toward the stairs. Then she hesitated and turned back. "We will come back in time for my engagement party, yes?" she asked her father. He didn't answer. He just pointed again toward the stairs and then turned to speak to her younger twin brothers, who came running from the living room to find out what was happening.

Elena hurried up to her room, her heart pounding. Something was wrong. She could feel it. She wished with all her heart that Roberto—her betrothed—was here. But he was studying at the university, and she wouldn't see him until he came home for their engagement party. Perhaps there would be time to call him before they left.

Her mother came into the room as Elena tossed clothing into her suitcase. "Pack important things," her mother said quietly. "Your photo albums, grandmother's jewelry, the painting you made in art class last year."

Elena paused with a shirt in her hand, staring wide eyed at her mother. Why did she need to pack all those things for a quick trip to Miami? These were things that belonged at home, not in a suitcase. Elena felt a clutch of fear in her heart.

"Mama, what's happening?" she whispered.

Her mother swallowed hard. Alarmed, Elena realized that her mother was fighting tears. "Clothes aren't important, Elena," she said, avoiding the question. "Clothes can be replaced. Bring your grandmother's icon," she directed, gesturing to the lovely icon that had been handed down for generations in the family. Elena's grandmother had given it to her only granddaughter a few days before her death. It was Elena's most cherished possession, excepting only Roberto's engagement ring, which she wore on her finger.

Elena packed carefully, leaving behind most of her clothes in order to fit the carefully wrapped painting and icon. She added the framed picture of her and Roberto at the last minute, throwing away a pair of sandals she had never liked much so that it would fit into the suitcase. Then she locked the suitcase and carried it downstairs.

Her father and mother were packing the twins into the car with their suitcases when she stepped outside. Papa took her heavy case and put it into the trunk. Then he locked the front door and started the car.

"Where's Tulia?" Elena called anxiously from the back seat. Tulia was the much-loved family dog.

"Roberto's parents will take care of Tulia for us," her mother replied.

Relieved, Elena sat back against the seat and watched her father turn into the street. Her mother gazed back at the house as they departed, and Elena realized she was crying. Elena broke out into a cold sweat, and her hands started shaking. It was almost as if her mother didn't expect to see the house ever again, which was nonsense. Wasn't it?

Elena hugged herself tightly, rubbing her hands over her arms to calm the chills that were running through her. *Oh, Roberto; I wish you were here,* she thought. He would know what was going on. Roberto was smart. While Elena paid attention to her schoolwork and to the love triangles and other scandals among her school friends, Roberto paid attention to politics and business and the word on the street. They were opposites, which was why they fit each other so well. She would phone Roberto as soon as they got to Uncle Juan's house, Elena decided. Never mind the expense of the overseas call.

Elena began putting two and two together during the journey to Miami when she overheard her parents talking about Fidel Castro. She had paid more attention to Roberto than to the news about Castro's rebel army, but even she knew that Castro was now in charge of the new government. Her father, a university professor, had been very outspoken in his views against Castro. Was that why they were leaving Cuba?

Uncle Juan had a small house that was already filled to the rafters with his four children and his in-laws. It was a tight squeeze for Elena and her family, who were used to their large, spacious home in Cuba. Still, they managed somehow.

It swiftly became obvious to Elena that her parents were not going back to Cuba—not with all the terrible things the new government was doing. According to news from back home, Castro's government was seizing private property, nationalizing public utilities, tightening controls on the private sector, and closing down all opposition newspapers. Soon all radio and television stations were under state control, and no reliable news could be obtained that way.

Letters from Roberto were few and far between. His parents had lost their home at the same time the government had seized Elena's house. His family wanted to come to the United States, but their money was gone. They had a hard time making ends meet and could not afford to leave. Roberto assured Elena that he would come to Miami as soon as he could and that they would marry and make a new life for themselves in America.

Elena clung to that hope, even as she struggled to improve her English and graduate from the American high school. She found a job as a waitress to help support her family while they tried to make a new life in a new land. Ten months after they arrived in Miami, her father was able to move them out of Uncle Juan's house and into a place of their own, which made things much more comfortable for everyone.

Almost a year to the day on which they had fled Cuba, Elena had a strange dream. She dreamed that Roberto was pushing a small, ramshackle boat into the water with the help of his younger brother and their cousin under cover of night. They rowed out into the ocean as quietly as they could and then started the motor. There were a few duffle bags in the bottom of the boat and some food and water. The whole endeavor looked dangerous to Elena. The boat was leaking, and it was far too small to be daring the ocean waves. Roberto looked older than she remembered him, and there were new, grim lines around his eyes and mouth. He looked determined and a little bit scared. Elena wondered what he was doing, where he was going. Night fishing?

Unusual for Elena, she remembered her dream when she woke the next morning. It had seemed so real. And Roberto had looked so different from the way he looked in the framed picture that she had brought from her room in Cuba—the picture she kissed every night before bed. She went to work in a thoughtful frame of mind, wondering about her dream until the lunchtime crowd drove it out of her head.

The next night, she dreamed again. In her dream she saw Roberto and his companions sitting in the small boat under the light of the full moon. The motor was broken and leaking oil into the water. The boat was being pushed hither and thither by the ocean waves. The three men were shivering in the cool ocean breeze, and their supplies were running low. Occasionally they tried to make headway with the oars, but they weren't getting anywhere fast.

Elena could feel Roberto's thirst as if it were her own. His mouth was so very dry after a long day in the sun with no shade. But there was almost no water left. They had to ration it carefully, lest they die of thirst in the middle of the ocean. As she watched, Roberto reached into his pocket and pulled

DARK DREAMS

out a tattered picture—her picture. His longing for her was so intense that Elena cried out to him: "Roberto! Roberto!"

She was shaken awake by her mother, who had heard Elena calling out in her dream. Elena clung to her mother, tears rolling down her cheeks. She told her mother what she had seen in her dream.

"Roberto is trying to get to Florida," she explained. "But the boat engine has broken down and he's so thirsty, Mama. That was the worst part of the dream. I could feel his thirst!"

Elena broke down completely then, sobbing in her mother's arms until she fell asleep. In the morning she begged her parents to alert the Coast Guard to look for Roberto and his brother and cousin. Her father and mother promised to try.

That evening, a series of storms rolled in from the sea. As the black clouds roiled above the landscape, Elena clasped her rosary to her lips and prayed desperately for Roberto, somewhere out at sea. *Please, God,* she prayed. *Please keep him safe.*

The third dream started almost as soon as Elena closed her eyes that night. Roberto was adrift in the ocean, clinging to the wreckage of the small boat. There was no sign of his brother or his cousin. He was weak from hunger and thirst and was finding it hard to hold on to the fragile boards amid the fierce storm swells. On the horizon he could see lightning flashes and hear thunder. Another storm was coming.

Elena woke with her heart thundering in her chest. "Hang on, Roberto," she gasped aloud. "Hang on!" She ran into her parents' room, shook them awake, and told them what she had dreamt.

"We asked the Coast Guard to look for them," her father reassured her, rubbing his eyes sleepily. "If anyone can find them, it will be the Coast Guard."

"Pray God," whispered her mother.

Elena tossed and turned the rest of the night, worrying about Roberto and the storm and praying that God would bring her beloved to her side.

It was almost dawn when she was awakened from a light sleep by a voice calling her name. She rolled over and blinked sleepily. The voice had sounded like Roberto's voice. Had he made it to Miami? Elena sat up and saw Roberto standing at the foot of her bed. His clothes were soaking wet, and his eyes were sad. He didn't speak; he just looked at her tenderly and touched his fingers to his lips, as if blowing her a kiss. Then he vanished.

For a moment Elena lay frozen in her bed. A chill ran through her body as she realized what her vision meant. Roberto had drowned in the storm, and his spirit had come to tell her good-bye. She covered her face with her hands, curling into a ball and screaming aloud in pain and despair. Immediately her parents came running into her room, followed by her brothers. Through her sobs, she told them what she had seen, and they all crowded into bed with her, trying to comfort and reassure her. It was only a dream, they said, only a dream. But no one believed it.

Three days later, Roberto's body washed up on a small island off Key West amid the wreckage of a small boat. According to the Coast Guard, he had drowned after his boat was destroyed during a storm. The bodies of his brother and cousin were never found.

PART TWO
Powers of Darkness and Light

13

Tailybone

There once was an ornery old Cracker who lived in the back of beyond, out where the woods and the swamp all came together to make one heck of a mess. Not many folks lived in the swamplands, but old Cracker was a bit of a miser, and it suited him just fine. He lived in a small cabin with his three dogs, and he mostly lived off the land—whatever he could catch with a fishing pole or shoot with his rifle gun or dig up out of the land went into his stew pot and frying pan.

Once or twice a year, old Cracker would hike into the nearest town to get a huge bag of corn meal, but that's all the socializing he ever did. His only friends were a few fellers that passed his place once or twice a month while they were out hunting. They'd stop sometimes and chat about this and that, sometimes have a cup of tea with old Cracker while his dogs snuffled about their feet or rolled over for a belly rub.

Well, old Cracker was cooking up a fish stew in his pot one evening long about Christmastime when he heard a funny scratching sound coming from the floor under his cabin. He'd raised the cabin up a couple of feet on a platform to keep it free from the rainy season waters that sometimes overwhelmed the swamplands all around him, and a couple of the floorboards were so warped and broken that a big hole gaped in the floor near the wall. Old Cracker's dogs weren't disturbed by the scratching sound, so he figured it wasn't anything to worry about. Of course his dogs wouldn't notice a charging bear when there was fish stew cooking, so that was no help.

Old Cracker grabbed his ax, just in case it was a gator trying to get in, and watched as a long snout poked through the hole. It was followed by two feet with very long, very sharp claws. Old Cracker tensed his muscles and hefted up the ax at the sight of those claws. They didn't look like the feet of a gator, but those claws sure looked sharp enough to do damage to a body.

Behind old Cracker, his old dog Calico started whining in her throat. But when he glanced quickly at her, he saw that she was still staring longingly at the fish stew, which was bubbling nicely and sending a delicious smell all through the cabin. The flickering flames of the fire below the pot turned the walls a warm orange-gold and sent shadows dancing around the room. It was a right pretty sight, but old Cracker didn't notice it on account of the critter scratching its way through his floor.

In his moment of inattention, the creature had managed to squeeze itself into the room. When he looked back, old Cracker saw a short-legged creature with spiky black fur and a bare tail that looked like a gator had tried to breed with a black bear and a possum at the same time. The critter was all long snout, pricked ears, sharp claws, and an extremely long, well-muscled tail.

"Nobody asked you to come fer dinner," exclaimed old Cracker, raising his ax. He threw it at the creature, which whisked around and scrambled for the hole in the floor. The ax landed smack-dab on the end of its body, cutting off the long tail at the base as the creature slipped under the house and away. Old Cracker could hear its painful yelp as it fled.

Calico tore her attention away from the stew and wandered over to look at the long tail, but old Cracker shooed her away. There was some good meat on that tail, and he aimed to eat it. It might cook up even better than gator. So old Cracker roasted up the tail on the fire and gave his three dogs the fish stew to eat while he feasted on roast critter. That tail tasted mighty fine with some greens he'd found in the woods that morning. Old Cracker kind of hoped that critter would come around again so that he could eat the rest of it. Yum!

After washing out the stew pot and his few dishes, old Cracker yawned and stretched, scratched his long beard a couple of times, and then went to bed. Maybe in the morning he'd try to track down that crazy critter. It probably had died from shock after losing its tail. He just hoped a gator hadn't gotten to it first. With that thought, he rolled over and went to sleep.

A piece later—coulda been a couple minutes, coulda been a couple hours; old Cracker couldn't tell—there came a scratch-scratch-scratching noise from underneath the raised floor of the cabin. It sounded almost like that strange critter had come back. But that critter was probably dead by now. Maybe it was another one. Old Cracker sat up in bed, licking his lips. Just then, a squeaky voice called out, "Tailybone. Tailybone. Whose got my tailybone?"

Old Cracker blinked in surprise, and goose bumps crawled along his arms. Was this some kind of trick? What was under his cabin, and how in tarnation could it talk?

"You get along outta here, you hear? Get!" he shouted,

thinking it was probably a fool kid from the settlement, come to plague him.

"Who's got my tailybone?" the little voice squeaked sharply. The high-pitched sound grated on old Cracker's nerves, making his spine tingle. "I want my tailybone."

Suddenly old Cracker was afraid of the voice. It didn't sound human. Maybe it was a haint! Ghosts came around sometimes and talked to people—at least that's what folks said in town. Old Cracker never believed it until now. Then again, he'd never heard of a haint making a scratching noise.

"Ino, Uno!" he shouted for his dogs. "Come on, Calico! There's something under the cabin fer you to eat!"

He jumped out of his creaky old bed and flung open the cabin door. The dogs rushed outside, and a moment later he heard them barking excitedly as they chased the whatever-it-was out from under the cabin and all the way down to the far reaches of the swamp. "That'll learn ya," muttered old Cracker as he settled back into bed to get some shut-eye. No way would that critter be back after his dogs got through with it.

Old Cracker fell into a deep sleep, only to be jerked awake around midnight with his heart thumping madly and his ears straining to hear whatever it was that had waked him. He couldn't hear a sound. Not the croak of a bullfrog, not the hoot of an owl, not even the chirps and buzzes of night insects broke the silence. He couldn't even hear his dogs breathing.

"Uno, Ino? Is that you?" he murmured into the unusual stillness, keeping his voice low as chills ran up and down his skin. "Calico? Are ya there?"

Then he heard the scratch-scratching noise right outside the cabin door. Old Cracker froze in his bed, not daring to move or

TAILYBONE

breathe. Had the strange critter come back, or was it the wind blowing a branch against his house.

Then a squeaky little voice called, "Tailybone. Tailybone. I want my tailybone."

Old Cracker swallowed dryly, trying to get rid of the lump in his throat. Tailybone? What was a tailybone? For a moment, the picture of a long, meaty tail with no fur on it flashed through his mind. He could almost hear it sizzling as it roasted on the fire.

"You get along outta here, you hear? Get!" he called, making his voice as firm as he could in spite of his roiling stomach.

"I want my tailybone!" the voice wailed, getting higher and higher in pitch until it hurt old Cracker's ears.

"Uno, Ino!" he shouted desperately, clamping his hands over his ears. "Come on, Calico! Get 'im!" He hoped his dogs could hear him over the noise.

There came a wild barking sound from the back of the cabin, and he heard the creature scrambling off his porch as his three dogs bounded after it, giving chase. They were a ways down in the swamplands when the barking broke off abruptly. Too abruptly. Old Cracker tensed, his ears straining. Had something happened to his dogs? The strange silence had fallen again around the cabin. Nothing stirred, nothing hummed or buzzed or chirped or hooted. Even the wind was silent.

Old Cracker's flesh creeped. "T'aint natural," he said of the silence as he crawled back into bed. He hoped his dogs had trapped that critter in a hole and that was why they'd stopped barking. But just in case, he slipped out of bed and barred the door. Then he stacked a couple of logs over the hole in the floor. These actions made him feel better, and he was almost cheerful as he crawled into bed. Nothing could get into the cabin with him now.

Just on the edge of sleep, he thought he heard a voice wafting up from the swamp. It said, "Tailybone. Tailybone. I'm gonna get my tailybone." He shivered a little, even as he drifted into deeper sleep.

In the darkness just before dawn, old Cracker woke again, startled by the sudden jarring of the bed. His whole body broke into a cold sweat, and his heart banged so hard it hurt his ribs.

"Wh . . . whose there?" he gasped in a voice that trembled so much he didn't recognize it as his own. He saw two glowing green lights appear at the foot of his bed, and something heavy landed suddenly on his feet, making the whole bed shake. Old Cracker grabbed hold of the mattress and tried to haul himself upright, hoping to flee, but the critter had him pinned down. He could feel its sharp claws pricking his skin as it walked up his body.

"Tailybone," it whispered. "Tailybone. I want my tailybone."

Old Cracker could feel blood dripping down his legs from the scratches ripped into his flesh by the creature's claws. He was panting so hard he thought his lungs would burst. He had to do something; say something. Anything . . .

"I ain't got yer tailybone!" he screamed in sheer, mind-crushing terror.

"Yes you DO!" screeched the creature. And it ripped out old Cracker's throat with one swipe of its claws.

When a passing hunter dropped by the cabin a few days later, he found a heap of bloody bones and some gristle, which was all that remained of old Cracker. He never did locate the man's tailbone.

Folks don't go back into that part of the swamp no more. Not even the hunters. They say the old stone fireplace still stands in the small clearing where old Cracker had his cabin. But nobody wants to go there on account of the voice that they hear sometimes in the wind calling out, "Now I GOT my tailybone! Tailybone . . . "

14

Little Lucy

A tall, proud figure was the medicine man. They said he was descended from an African princess who married a Native American warrior-priest, and he looked the part. There was a regal air about him, with his dark hair and flashing eyes that could pierce like the gaze of an eagle. His thin face seemed cold and proud—until he smiled. People who earned a smile from the medicine man would follow him to the ends of the earth ever afterward, so they said. It was that kind of smile.

The medicine man wore the ordinary trousers, shirt, and coat that any man living in a Florida settlement might have worn, but added to these were two items that were not typical. One was a sheathed knife he wore strapped around his calf. It had a green jewel in the hilt, and when the medicine man was working, the jewel was said to glow with an unearthly light. The second item hung from a thong around his neck. It was a small pouch that was said to contain the dust of the warrior-priests from whom he descended. This dust was so powerful that he needed only a pinch of it to work wonders. Or so they said in the local settlements.

Normally the young couple working a small farm on the outer reaches of the remote settlement would never have dreamed of approaching such an awesome figure as the medicine man. But terrible fear moved them as nothing else would. For their only daughter—the light of their eyes—lay dying on her bed, wasting away day after day. And no one knew why.

She was a scamp of a little girl with golden blond curls and big green eyes, who had never been sick a day in her life. She raced around the farm with her little dog, Lucy, climbing trees, building forts, petting the farm animals, making friends with the wild birds, and singing her little heart out—mostly songs she made up about her dog. "Lucy Lu. My friend Lu. Lucy Lu's a darling," she caroled over and over, until both her parents were singing it too.

And little Lucy was a darling. She weighed all of ten pounds, just a wee mite of a dog with black curls all over her minute body. But she made up for her tiny size with her fierce spirit and protective ways. She wasn't afraid of anything and would do whatever it took to protect her family, especially her beloved mistress. Little Lucy would bark at gators if they got too close to the house, scold the workhorses when they got too lazy, growl when she saw snakes, and chase away much larger dogs if they set foot on her property. And nobody who seemed threatening got anywhere near her golden-haired little mistress. She was the perfect watchdog.

But even Lucy couldn't save her friend from the mysterious malady that overtook her. One day the little girl came into the house, complaining that she was tired. She lay down on her little bed and couldn't get up again. Her poor little body became rigid, as if she were made of wood. And her arms curled inward until they lay shriveled and useless across her tiny chest, which barely moved, so tiny were her breaths. Little Lucy lay on the bed beside

LITTLE LUCY

her young mistress, keeping watch and occasionally licking her cheek. But she could do nothing to help her little friend.

The parents were terrified when they saw this transformation of their previously healthy little daughter. The father went all the way to the next settlement to fetch the doctor, but old Doc could find nothing wrong with her. He stayed at their farm for several days, doing everything he could to cure her using traditional medicine, but the little girl just faded more and more into her own head, her skin growing paler and translucent, her body more rigid, her eyes vacant. Finally the doctor told the grieving parents to prepare themselves for the worst. He left them several bottles of medicine, and the husband drove him back to the settlement, for the doctor had other patients to tend whom he had neglected for too long.

The mother sat beside her daughter's bed, stroking her shriveled arm as she waited for her husband to return home with the wagon. There must be something they could do, she thought desperately. They couldn't just let their little girl die without a fight. The tired mother cudgeled her brain, trying to find some hope for her daughter. By the time she heard the jingle of the harness and the thud of hooves in the farmyard, signaling the arrival of her husband, she had remembered the stories she'd heard about the medicine man. Excited, she hurried out to the farmyard to speak to her husband. Little Lucy caught her excitement and followed her outside for the first time in days, barking with something of her old spirit.

"It will be hard to find him," the young father said. "He roams to all the settlements in turn, and I'm not sure which tribe he lives with when he's not roaming."

But the young father was determined to try. It gave him something to do, and action was better than sitting at home, waiting for his daughter to die. So he saddled up a fresh horse and rode to all the nearby settlements to leave messages for the medicine man. It took him three days to return, and his daughter had faded away to practically nothing in his absence. Her mother couldn't get any food down her throat and only a few sips of water. It looked like the end.

And then little Lucy lifted her head from her mistress's pillow and whined, looking toward the window. Suddenly she sprang up and raced out of the room, barking a welcome. She danced in front of the door until the father let her out, and then she raced into the yard to dance around the tall, mysterious figure of the medicine man. The medicine man smiled at the little dog—a smile that made you want to follow him to the ends of the earth—and he picked her up and scratched her faithful little head as he stepped into the house.

Tremulously the young parents took the medicine man to see their daughter. He placed little Lucy on the bed beside her young mistress and then spent several minutes examining the little girl from every angle. Finally he took the parents to the kitchen and instructed them to go outside and pick wildflowers, keeping positive thoughts of healing in their minds while they worked. The parents agreed at once and looked at each other in hope for the first time since their daughter had fallen ill.

As they left the property in search of wildflowers, the medicine man began his rituals. He opened the windows and doors to let in the fresh air. Then he went outside the house, pulling sacred objects out of his conjure bag and ritually marking the front door before he began the sacred ritual for summoning healing forces that were known only to a few of his people. As he worked, the clouds overhead began to boil and swirl. Then a fierce wind swept through the farmyard, trying to flatten everything in its path. But the medicine man continued chanting until the wind died away and a single ray of light beamed down through the shadows. The ray of light was followed by others as the clouds parted and blue sky shown through. When the farmyard was ablaze with sunlight, the medicine man released the first part of his healing ritual. The second part would begin when the child's parents returned.

A few minutes passed in peace and calm. A gentle, warm breeze filled the clearing, and the air outside the farmhouse buzzed with light and hope for the first time in weeks. When the parents returned with their offering of wildflowers, the medicine man had them stand outside the open windows and sing a sacred song while he continued the healing rituals inside the house.

Taking the armful of flowers from the mother, he walked inside the house. Instantly the small house began to shake as if it were caught up in a massive earthquake. As he strewed handfuls of flowers on the kitchen table and floor, the shaking grew worse. Pots and pans rattled and cutlery jumped in its drawer as he stepped into the child's bedroom. As he strewed flowers around her bed, the shaking grew so bad that the small mirror on the wall shattered and little Lucy sat up in alarm, her dark eyes watching him keenly. The little dog trembled from head to toe, frightened by the shaking, but she refused to leave her mistress's side. The medicine man gave her a pat on the head as he strewed the last of the flowers around the child on the bed.

Then he began a ritual chant of healing, calling for the Powers to rescue this child from the darkness that threatened her life. Suddenly the little girl stiffened and sat bolt upright, her eyes staring blankly into nothing. Her mouth opened and a black mist boiled out, filling the room with a foul stench. Two red lights appeared at the back of the child's throat, and the evil head of a black serpent appeared, tapping its way forward along her tongue. Slowly the medicine man tempted the serpent forth, offering it mushroom caps bespelled to make them irresistible to a spirit creature such as the one that dwelled in the child. The serpent slid slowly out of the child's mouth as she made miserable retching sounds in her throat. It was nearly as long as the child's body, and the medicine man was amazed that the child was still alive with such a dark being in possession of her. She must be a very strong and honorable child indeed to fight so long against such a spirit.

Suddenly the serpent was loose on the bed. This was the moment of danger. The medicine man reached for his special knife with the jewel in the hilt. But his fingers had not quite reached it before the serpent sprang forward and coiled its body around him, squeezing tight. The medicine man cried out, the knife dropping to the floor. The evil spirit squeezed tighter, cutting off his breath. Then the evil serpent thrust its head into his mouth, intent on possessing him as it had possessed the child.

On the bed, little Lucy started yapping fiercely, dancing around the covers and over the little girl's legs as she nipped again and again at the snake's black body. The medicine man made frantic sounds in his throat and thrust out his chest so that the medicine bag full of the dust of the warrior-priests swung out from under his shirt. Little Lucy made a great leap and tore the bag off its thong. The mouth of the bag gaped open and dust spilled out over the bed, over the little girl, over the choking medicine man, and over the evil serpent spirit.

The skin of the evil spirit began to sizzle. It withdrew its red-eyed head from the medicine man and screamed—an inhuman wail that cut through the soul like razor blades. Wherever the dust landed, the serpent's skin boiled and turned into a black mist. Within seconds, the serpent shape had vanished and a small dark cloud roiled above the bed. With a gasp of command, the medicine man scooped up the last of the dust and threw it into the cloud, which vanished with a bang.

The young parents came bursting fearfully into the house, having heard the serpent's terrible scream. A wave of fresh air, perfumed by flowers and filled with the hope conjured by the first part of the ritual, filled the child's bedroom.

The medicine man was already getting to his feet, and on the bed little Lucy was ecstatically licking the face of her young mistress. The child's eyes were closed, but her parents could hear her singing very softly: "Lucy Lu. My friend Lu. Lucy Lu's a darling."

Then she opened her green eyes and looked up at her weeping parents. Her mother gathered up the child and hugged her tightly, and the father—forgetting himself in his joy—pounded the medicine man on the back, just as he would have done to one of his buddies at the tavern.

The medicine man gave him one of his rare smiles, but the father backed away hastily, remembering that the man was descended from an African princess and a warrior-priest. But such was the power of the medicine man's smile that the father relaxed and smiled back before hurrying forward to pull mother and child into his arms.

The medicine man silently withdrew from the house, pausing only to collect the sacred items he'd used in the healing ritual. When he reached the yard, he heard a short bark behind him. Turning, he saw little Lucy running down the steps toward him. She carried his leather pouch in her mouth. Smiling, he knelt down and rubbed the little dog behind the ears before taking the pouch from her. There was still a little dust in the very bottom of the pouch, so he pulled the straps tightly and reached up to secure it to the thong around his neck. Then he paused as a thought struck him. He looked into the eyes of the faithful little dog, who would continue to guard her susceptible little mistress when he was gone. She might need some help keeping evil spirits away from her mistress in the future, and he might not always be around to help.

He lowered his arms and beckoned to the dog. She jumped at once into his lap, and he laughed as he fended off her joyful licks. Then he tied the bag around the collar of little Lucy as she wagged her stubby tail and wriggled in delight. When he was finished, she licked his cheek, giving a meaty "woof" of thanks into his ear.

"Lucy Lu. My friend Lu. Lucy Lu's a darling," the medicine man said softly, stroking her tiny head as she joyfully rolled her eyes. Then he shooed the dog back into the house to tend her mistress and left the sunny farmyard to the laughing, shouting, weeping voices of its rejoicing family—and to the excited yapping of a very special little dog.

Roses

In the end, what enraged him more than the love affair itself was the way they assumed he had the intelligence of a wooden post. Did they think he wouldn't notice the way his wife lit up whenever his first officer entered the room or the way the first officer followed her with his eyes? Obviously they thought he was too stupid to realize how they both just happened to disappear at the same time and that when they reappeared, she was glowing and his uniform smelled of rose perfume. It was infuriating!

His father had warned him against taking such a flirtatious, pretty woman to wife. She would stray, he had said, and, devil curse him, his father had been right. And his men were laughing at him behind his back. They knew what was going on. Oh, yes they did. He was a laughingstock because of his wife and his first officer, and it was going to stop tonight. He would make sure of it.

When his wife swept into his commandant's quarters in the Castillo, he was seated at his desk, apparently absorbed in paperwork. She had been pouting for days, ever since he'd sent his first officer south to the Caribbean with an important commission that would keep him away from the Castillo for more than two years. She flounced into a chair and glared at him in petty anger.

"Well?" she said peevishly when he refused to look up. He glanced at the door and nodded to the night guard who stood there. The man tactfully withdrew from the room, closing the heavy door behind him.

He leaned back in his chair, his nostrils twitching as the cloying scent of her rose perfume filled the room. "Well, my dear. It seems we are at an impasse," he said. "I am happy working in this New World, but you are not happy living here. Or should I say you are not happy living here with me?"

His wife looked up sharply, going a little pale at the tone of his voice. She searched his eyes, trying to see what, if anything, he knew about her and her lover.

"What nonsense have you got in your head?" she asked, trying to sound playful—and failing. "I am perfectly happy here with you!"

"You have not seemed so these last few months," said the commandant. He rose from his seat and beckoned to his wife. "However, perhaps the surprise I have for you will mend matters. Come, walk with me."

"A surprise for me?" asked his wife, half delighted and half suspicious.

She rose with a dubious smile on her red lips, and he bowed her through the door into the outer chamber, where the night guard stood to attention.

As the commandant took his wife's arm, he said loudly, "There is a ship in the harbor that leaves for Spain at first light, my dear. I am sure the captain would be happy to oblige us when we explain the situation to him."

His wife gave him a puzzled glance at this sudden change of

topic, but it was not for her benefit that he broached it. He saw the guard start a little and then school his face to impassivity as they swept out into the courtyard, arm in arm. The commandant smiled grimly. The night guard would certainly pass along what he'd heard to the other men, fueling the speculation about the commandant and his unfaithful wife.

"What was all that about a ship?" his wife demanded petulantly as they crossed the courtyard.

"It's all part of the surprise," he told her soothingly as he led her to an unused storeroom and escorted her inside.

"Why are we here?" his wife demanded sharply, staring at the broken pieces of furniture and dusty wooden crates that filled the room. "This is no place to hide a gift."

"On the contrary, my dear," said the commandant happily. "It is the perfect place to hide something."

So saying, he led her to a concealed opening in the wall. His wife stared at it. "What is that?" she asked suspiciously. "Why have I never seen it before?"

"It is a hidden room I discovered some time ago," said the commandant. "It is a place to store secret things."

He lifted the torch from its socket beside the storeroom door and went to the dark opening. With a smile, he gestured for his wife to precede him into the secret room. The scent of her rose perfume filled the air as she stepped inside to see her surprise.

At dawn the next morning, the commandant stood on the pier, waving good-bye to the ship bound for Spain. When the ship disappeared over the horizon, he strolled thoughtfully back to the Castillo and explained to his men that his wife had left for Spain to tend her ailing father. The soldiers exchanged looks, but none of them said anything in front of him. However, he

ROSES

knew that among themselves they would spread a different tale—one that claimed the commandant had discovered his wife's affair with the first officer and had separated the lovers, sending the officer to the Caribbean and banishing her to Spain for her infidelity. The commandant didn't care what the gossips said. What mattered was that his unfaithful wife and her lover were gone, and he was a free man.

A few months later, the commandant resigned his position and left the Castillo for good. He left behind only vague rumors about his wife's scandalous love affair that had gone awry.

Fifty years swiftly passed away, and the story of the commandant's unfaithful wife had faded from the memory of the townspeople. Florida was now part of the United States, and the Castillo had become Fort Marion. New faces and new concerns filled the stone rooms and towers, and one of those faces belonged to Sergeant Tuttle. On this particular day, his main concern was moving some old cannons around the upper gun deck, not an easy task at the best of times.

"Heave," he told his men.

"Heave!" they answered, doing so.

CRASH went the cannon, right through the floor.

"Holy Moses!" shouted Tuttle, staring down into the huge hole that had opened in the floor of the gun deck. He could barely make out the cannon at the bottom amidst the dust, debris, and filtered sunlight. "What a god-awful mess! You men, get down there right now!" he added, pointing to the two men closest to the stairs.

The men hurried down the stairs and into the room below the gun deck, only to find it devoid of debris. There was no mess, no cannon, no dust. Nothing was amiss.

The men stared wide eyed at each other and then checked the adjoining rooms. Still nothing. Where was the dang-blasted cannon?

The two men ran back up to the gun deck to inform Tuttle of the disappearing cannon. The sergeant, still staring down the hole, commented that it was taking his men far too long to appear. He jumped a mile when one of them spoke at his elbow.

"Sarge, we can't find the cannon," the man reported. Tuttle jerked upright and whirled around. "What do you mean you can't find the cannon?" he roared. "It's right there!" He gestured into the hole.

"It may be right there," said the man, quaking but defiant, "but it isn't down there!" He gestured to the room below. The two men dragged Tuttle downstairs and showed him the empty room. By this time, most of the men working on the gun deck had followed them downstairs, so there was quite a crowd when the sergeant pronounced, "There must be a sealed chamber behind that wall. Men, we need pickaxes and sledgehammers."

Immediately the soldiers dispersed to locate the requested tools, and soon several men were hammering away at the coquina wall with a will, speculating between blows about the reason the newly christened cannon room had been sealed.

As the first hammer penetrated the secret room, the air was suddenly filled with an overwhelming scent of roses. A moment later, the hole was big enough to peer inside. The men ripped away at the hole until there was room to enter the hidden chamber. Grabbing a lantern, Tuttle stepped into the secret space, followed by his men. There, amid the dust and rubble, stood the fallen cannon. And behind it, chained to the wall, were two moldering skeletons. One still wore the decaying remains of a first officer's uniform. The other still smelled faintly of roses.

106

16

The Watermelon Thief

GAINESVILLE

When my wife and I retired, I agreed to move to Florida on one condition: that we purchase a yard big enough for me to grow my prize-winning watermelons. My wife, who was sick of living in the Snowbelt, promptly agreed. She, even more promptly, had half our back lawn plowed up as soon as we moved in and planted a huge kitchen garden, along with a rose trellis and more flowers than you could shake a stick at. It was real pretty, smelled wonderful—what with all those herbs—and was downright useful come suppertime. But because watermelon vines can grow up to twelve feet in all directions, there wasn't a bit of space left for my watermelons. That made me mad. My wife's a cantaloupe person—something I didn't know until after we were married, mind you! You can't expect a cantaloupe person to appreciate what it takes to grow prize-winning watermelons. They just don't have it in them.

Fortunately for our marriage, there was a spare lot right next door going a-begging. It was more money than I wanted to pay, but I bought it anyway. It was that or get rid of the missus. (After forty-five years, I figured I'd better keep her around.) Soon as the paperwork was signed, I was out there turning the soil and preparing it for my crop.

Now growing giant watermelons ain't easy. First I had to consider what variety of watermelon I wanted to grow. Variety selection is one of the most important decisions made by the grower. The Carolina Cross watermelons I grew in Ohio might not work so well in Florida. That was the first thing I had to find out. Florida had a humid climate, and foliar diseases were more prevalent here. I had to be especially on the lookout for a couple of nasties called anthracnose race 1 and fusarium wilt.

I spent a lot of time with the local farmers, shooting the breeze and talking watermelons over the next few weeks. By the time the spare lot was ready to plant, I'd decided to take a chance on growing my Carolina Cross watermelons and see how it went. At one of the big farm shows last year, a Carolina Cross had topped two hundred pounds. Hot diggity dog!

The best time to plant in north Florida is between February 15 and early April. I was right out there February 15, raring to go. Of course from that moment on, it's a battle with Mother Nature. Aside from the diseases your young plants can get, there's also a wide variety of insects that like eating watermelon plants. Then you've got to get the fertilization and the irrigation just right. Yep, that water is real important. Too much can leach nutrients or promote disease. But too little can stress your watermelons, and that reduces fruit size and quality.

It's not easy growing a winner, let me tell you. But my watermelon plants were thriving, mostly due to the diligent watch I kept over my crop. I had an early run-in with cucumber bugs, but I managed to get them under control before they impacted the whole crop. And only one of my plants succumbed to that pesky fusarium wilt, which was just plain luck.

I spent quite a bit of time in our spare lot that first year. More than I thought, apparently. My wife, Hannah, started complaining that I was spending more time with my watermelons than with her. Of course I could have said the same thing about her tomatoes, but I refrained for purposes of marital harmony. Instead I cut down a few palm trees that were standing between the two properties so that we could see each other clearly when we were out working in our separate gardens. Such sacrifices are necessary to the ebb and flow of happily married life. We even set up a romantic little gazebo between the two lots, where we could sit on white wicker furniture having our morning coffee and enjoying the scents from my wife's herb garden and the sight of my giant watermelons, which were plumping up nicely next door.

I'd planted watermelons three times during the season, one batch each month, so I'd have a nice harvest all summer long. The first batch had a couple of forty pounders, and one of the melons in batch 2 looked like it might top one hundred pounds. But batch 3 was the one in which I set all my hopes. There were a couple of hundred pounders in the making and a third watermelon I nicknamed Theo (don't ask me why, that's the name that came to me while I was hoeing) that was going to go all the way—maybe even two hundred pounds. Hot dog!

We picked our first watermelon at the end of May, and even Hannah had to admit it was almost perfect. She ate it two mornings in a row, forgoing her usual cantaloupe. I can't ask for a better reward than that. We gave away a couple of the smaller melons over the next few weeks, and word started spreading that we had the tastiest watermelons in town. I didn't have too many melons to spare, since most of my concentration was going into growing the giants in batch 3, but we did invite the neighbors over when the first hundred-pound watermelon was ready to harvest.

You can tell a watermelon's ready when the ground spot changes from pale green or white to cream or yellow. The tendrils near the fruit stem will dry and turn brown. Folks came from all over our neighborhood to attend the event (more than we'd invited, by a long shot, but we didn't care). Everyone cheered when I thumped the side of that hundred-pounder. The sound of a watermelon when thumped with a finger is a muffled, dull tone if it is ripe, and this melon was ripe!

I needed help carrying it over to the gazebo, where Hannah and a few ladies from church were ready with carving knives, plates, and plastic forks and spoons (for the squeamish who didn't want to bite right in). Oh, my, that was a very good day!

A week later, I wasn't feeling so happy. One of the hundred-pound watermelons from batch 3 had gone missing during the night.

"It's too durned easy, Hannah!" I stormed, marching up and down the rows between her tomato plants. "That spare lot backs right up against state parkland. Anyone can slip in and steal a watermelon!"

"If you don't want it to happen again, you'd better build a fence," Hannah said, sitting back on her heels and wiping her sweaty forehead with a dusty glove.

"Good idea! That's just what I'm going to do!" I said, heading toward the garage at once. "Keep an eye on Theo," I shouted over my shoulder. By my estimation, Theo was already 150 pounds and still growing. I was lucky the watermelon thief hadn't taken him. Too heavy, I guess. He'd need a truck—or at least a handcart!

A few of my buddies from around the neighborhood helped me set up a large wire fence between the state park and the back of the spare lot, posted with KEEP OUT signs. A few feet inside that fence and all around the rest of the lot, we put up a quaint-looking white picket fence that spruced up the lot while providing marginal protection from watermelon thieves. I was passionate about my watermelons, but I didn't want to be accused of bringing down the tone of our neighborhood; not when everyone was so nice and friendly.

The picket fence looked great with the white gazebo, and I got a bit carried away and laid down gravel walkways between the watermelon plots. Hannah planted climbing vines and rose bushes to further enhance the garden. It took us more than a week, but by the time we were done, that spare lot was a showplace. Hannah even talked me into putting a fancy water fountain in the center. She also put a couple reflecting balls here and there among the vines, and I installed benches at either end of the walkway. Visitors started stopping by to gaze longingly into the garden, it looked so nice.

Fortunately all this activity around the garden seemed to have scared away the watermelon thief. Or maybe it was all the fencing. Anyway, no more watermelons were stolen, and a week after I put in the benches, we had another block party to celebrate the cutting of a 120-pounder from batch 3. We served champagne this time, which was a big hit, and everyone toasted Big Theo, which, by my estimation, was now a solid 175 pounds.

The next night, another watermelon was stolen. This one weighed 130 pounds, so the thief (or thieves) must have been very strong to cart it away without us hearing anything from

THE WATERMELON THIEF

the house. (I'd been sleeping with the window open every night since the first theft!) I studied the ground around the watermelon patch carefully but couldn't see much. It had been very dry recently, and we'd had a lot of people milling about the previous day, so I couldn't tell which prints were those of a visitor and which a thief. I didn't see any wheelbarrow or handcart tracks, so that possibility was ruled out.

I was all set to install a fancy alarm system, but Hannah persuaded me to take the cheap route first. So I went to the fancy gift store and got a whole set of jingle bells and attached them underneath the vines around all the remaining watermelons, and I triple-belled Big Theo. "That should scare any thieves away," I said to Hannah when I finished. "And it will give us plenty of warning too."

I put my baseball bat next to the back door, just in case, before I went to sleep that night. But nary a bell woke us, and all the watermelons were there in the morning. After a week of restless sleep, I relaxed my guard a little, though I kept the baseball bat by the back door.

Then one night I was awakened by a ferocious jangling sound coming from the spare lot.

"Someone's stealing Big Theo," I roared, leaping out of bed before I had my eyes properly open. I thundered downstairs and grabbed the baseball bat, waving it to and fro as I charged through the back door and out onto the moonlit lawn.

"Step away from the watermelon!" I shouted as I plunged past the gazebo. I could see a dark figure bending over Big Theo as I leapt the white picket fence with the baseball bat, ready to do battle. The figure straightened up, and I caught a whiff of rotten garbage smell that made my nose wrinkle in disgust. Then the figure straightened up some more, with Big Theo gripped in its giant hands. It had to be more than eight feet tall!

I got a good look at it in the moonlight—and stopped dead beside the burbling fountain. It was hairy all over, with long arms that ended in huge hands. The huge feet at the bottom of its long, hairy legs were bare. Its face was humanoid but flattened, and its huge dark eyes were staring warily at me as Hannah charged past the gazebo. She paused by the picket fence when she caught sight of the large figure silhouetted against the moonlight.

I drew in a long, shaky breath and then said to the skunk ape, "You drop that watermelon at once, do you hear?" I waved the baseball bat, but it was a feeble gesture. Big Theo was at least 180 pounds by now. Any creature that could lift 180 pounds so easily wouldn't be frightened by my baseball bat.

The skunk ape made a funny grunting sound, almost like a laugh. Then it whirled around and loped away into the state park, easily leaping both picket and barbed-wire fence.

As I collapsed against the edge of the fountain, panting heavily, Hannah said, "Dear Lord, was that what I thought it was?"

"If you thought it was a skunk ape, also known as Sasquatch or Bigfoot, then you thought right," I said, dragging myself upright.

"And he just stole Big Theo," Hannah said indignantly.

"You got that right too," I said, throwing the baseball bat on the ground in disgust. "Just before the growers contest too. Dang it, Hannah! I thought we left Sasquatches back in Ohio. Who'd have guessed they'd be down here stealing watermelons!"

Hannah stopped muttering to herself and started to chuckle. I glared at her a moment in the moonlight, and then I started to chuckle too. I walked over to the picket fence and we clung together, laughing and kissing in the moonlight. I was still durned mad, but what an experience!

"You realize no one is going to believe this," Hannah said when we'd both calmed down.

"Nope. We'll just have to say it was the watermelon thief again," I agreed, using the gate this time to exit the garden. "But I tell you what, Hannah. I'm going to the pound tomorrow morning and getting me a dog! Otherwise, we won't have any more watermelons to eat this summer!"

"I'll come with you," Hannah said at once. "After all, when your watermelons are done, there will still be plenty of cantaloupes left. And a melon's a melon, especially if you're a skunk ape."

"Ha! I disagree," I said, opening the back door for my wife of forty-five years. "Your cantaloupes can't hold a candle to my watermelons!"

It was an argument we'd been having since the first days of our marriage, and we bickered amiably all the way back to bed. The next day we got a dog, and that was the last we saw of the watermelon thief. And the next year I grew a two-hundred-pound watermelon and won first prize at the state fair. So all's well that ends well!

17

True Love

He had been searching for his True Love for many years—in Europe, in Australia, and in the United States. He had a vision of his True Love when he was twelve years old, back in 1889. He had seen a raven-haired beauty in a white dress with huge, speaking dark eyes, and he had fallen in love at once. But hunt as he might, his True Love never appeared. He eventually married but finally separated from his wife, the vision of his True Love ever before his eyes. It was after the breakup with his spouse that he came to America and found her, where he least expected to.

He was working as an X-ray technologist in Key West when she came through the door, weary with illness and yet lovely still. He recognized her at once from his long-ago vision. It was she—his True Love! She had suffered much during her sickness, losing first an unborn child and then a husband, who ran off rather than support her.

She was very young, he saw as he did her X-rays—twenty-three to his fifty-one. No wonder he had not met her before. But he could see she had a good heart, and she was fighting with all her might to conqueror her illness. He wondered what she made of him—a tall, spindly man with a pointed gray

116

beard and a German accent. He wondered if she knew they were destined for each other.

In the days that followed, he made the acquaintance of her family and supported her through her sickness in every way he could. He even proposed marriage, but he could see it was too soon for her. She was still mourning the no-good man who had left her, and she needed her remaining energy to keep her fighting her sickness. So he bided his time patiently, knowing that fate would eventually bring them together.

More trouble came, and with it pain and loss. He became a tower of strength to his True Love's family, paying for everything that was needed, attending religious ceremonies with them, even renting a room in the family home so they had extra income to help them through. He would often go to the cemetery to honor the one they had lost. In his heart, he knew that his time had come. His True Love would be with him forever very soon.

He finally found a place of his own and moved out of the house. But he continued courting his True Love, bringing her gifts and flowers, singing to her. He told her all about his new house. It was the perfect place. He'd had the shell of a wingless airplane placed in the yard. His True Love would like it, he knew. To him it represented the glory of love. He would make her well, and the wingless plane would fly them to heaven! It was a fanciful thing to say, but she liked it. He brought her to live in his new home so that he could help make her well. When she was good as new—perhaps even a little better, for love can transform a person—he married her.

He was happier than he'd ever been in his life; discussing everything under the sun with his True Love, playing music

TRUE LOVE

and dancing with her, showering her with gifts, and delighting in the mysterious half smile upon her lips. This was heaven! A hard-won heaven, it was true, but heaven nonetheless.

They had eight glorious years together before trouble came for them yet again. This time it came in the form of his True Love's sister. Some people cannot stand to see others be happy, and it seemed that the sister fell into this category. She claimed that he was a monster. That he was desecrating his True Love! It was a lie, but she believed it utterly, even after she had seen for herself how happy his True Love was. The sister even uttered an ultimatum: Part now, or she would go to the police. She gave them five days to comply with her wishes before she went to the authorities with her tale. It was something out of his worst nightmares.

He discussed the matter with his True Love that night. Perhaps they could fool the sister and the authorities—pretend to go along with them and then flee together for a more salubrious place where they could live together in peace. He pondered long into the night and finally came up with a plan he thought would work. He told the plan to his True Love and again basked in the mysterious half smile on her lips. Yes, it was a good plan.

The police believed the sister, and the man was arrested and put on trial. Fortunately the minute details of the law were in his favor, and his case was dismissed. The enforced separation from his True Love was traumatic for him, and her family still stood between them. Disheartened, he moved to Zephyrhills to be near his sister, taking his wingless airplane with him. And there his True Love joined him, just as they had planned. By this time, age was catching up with him. His True Love looked just as young and beautiful as the day he had married her, but he was old and tired. So tired.

On the last day of his life, he lay down next to his True Love and held her in his arms, delighting one last time in the beautiful waxen face, the carefully molded smile. Only a few hours now and he would be with his Elena at last, he thought. She would no longer be the corpse that he had stolen from her mausoleum after she died of tuberculosis and carefully preserved in the laboratory he set up in the fuselage of the wingless airplane. Nor would she be this carefully molded life-size doll he had made after the police had taken her body away from him. His time on Earth was ending, and his soul would wing its way to paradise, where the soul and spirit of his Elena awaited him. He clutched the doll a little closer to him, laid his head down, and died.

18

The Hermit

When I was a little girl, folks in the settlement used to warn us children not to go near the hermit who roamed the swamplands near our home. He was an old man; tall and thin with a scraggly gray beard. He wore a faded and torn gingham dress with a snakeskin belt around his waist and an old sunbonnet on his head. He carried a rifle in his huge hands, and the look of dark intensity in his eyes prevented folks from teasing him about his strange attire.

I was afeard of the hermit and hid behind my widowed mama's skirts whenever he came to town to buy supplies, which didn't happen too often. Sometimes I'd have nightmares in which the hermit chased me round and round our cabin until I woke up screaming.

When I was eight years old, some of the local boys started teasing me in the street of the town. When I stuck up for myself, the biggest of the boys pushed me down into the dirt. Afore I could do more than gasp, the hermit appeared, towering over me and the boys. I was so scared I almost soiled my skirts, but the hermit weren't after me. He was right furious at the boys, and he grabbed up the big bully that pushed me down and gave him what-for until the bully ran off crying, followed by his gang. Then the old man picked me up, dusted me off, and took me home to my mama. From that moment on, whenever anyone talked mean about the hermit, I defended him. He might dress strange, but he had a good heart, and I liked him.

The year I turned ten, I was out in one of the local meadows picking flowers for my mama when I found the hermit sitting on a stump carving a piece of wood into a beautiful statue of a blue heron. He didn't look up, even when I stopped to watch him work. He just kept carving with those big, wrinkled hands of his, the curling pieces of wood falling all over his worn-out gingham dress.

I watched him carve for a long time. I was fascinated by the way the heron appeared out of the rough piece of wood, smooth and sleek as anything. It was amazing. As I turned to go, I lay the prettiest flower I'd found on the stump beside the hermit. I was a few yards away when the old man called gruffly, "What's your name, little girl?"

"Emma," I said. "I'm called Emma."

A few weeks later I found a beautiful, sleek carving of a blue heron on our porch with my name carved into the bottom. It was the loveliest thing I had ever owned, and I put it in a place of honor on the fireplace mantle where Mama and I could both enjoy it.

I walked three miles to the hermit's backwoods cabin to say thank you. I found the old man chopping wood as sturdily as a man half his age, his sunbonnet hanging down his back from its ribbons, which were tied around his wrinkled neck. He was chatting to an enormous pet alligator that lived in a pool near the house.

His cabin was made of slabs, and outside the door was a chair made from a cypress knee. I caught a glimpse of a heap of raw cotton inside the doorway that might have been his bed, and the fire inside was burning on a flat stone. There were several gourds beside it carved out into rough dishes. I wondered why he used gourds when he could make beautiful woodcarvings like the heron. I didn't ask. I just gave the hermit my best curtsy, handed him the pie Mama had baked for him, and said "thank you" for the gift.

The hermit wiped his sweaty hands on his worn blue-gingham dress before accepting the pie from me. "Ya didn't have to do nothing," the old man growled, though I could tell he was pleased. His dark eyes lost their hard intensity and grew soft and brown, like my papa's eyes had been. Papa had died when I was six, but I still remembered his eyes.

"I helped make the piecrust," I said, sitting down on a big flat rock beside the cabin. "Are you going to give a piece to your alligator?"

"I don't reckon alligators like pie," said the hermit. "Do you want a piece, Devil?" he asked the monster in the green pool.

No one would ever believe me if I told them, but I swear that gator grinned at him with its ferocious teeth and shook its head back and forth. The hermit laughed when he saw the look of amazement on my face.

"Devil and I communicate very well," he said. I nodded, wide eyed.

"Would Devil like a chicken pie?" I asked. "Mama makes a right good chicken pie."

"Ask him," said the hermit.

THE HERMIT

I did, and that crazy gator nodded his huge head up and down. I don't know whether he really understood me or he was just responding to some signal from the hermit. Whichever the case, it was a good trick.

I came back a week later with two chicken pies, one for the hermit and one for Devil. Devil ate his in one gulp, and the hermit and I sat on the big, flat rock and shared the other. Timidly, I asked him about his dress, and he said it belonged to his wife, who had died. He looked so sad I didn't say anything else. But after a moment, he told me his story.

He had once lived with his family in a settlement in Georgia, but he had quarreled with a man named Morgan who was a direct descendant of the pirate called Morgan and a prominent man in that town. So the hermit had moved to Florida with his wife and son and had built a nice cabin on this very spot.

Several happy years passed, and then the hermit—who was called Jim Baines back then and had dressed like a normal man—chanced upon the man Morgan while he was out hunting in the woods. Visitors didn't often appear in this part of the state, and so the hermit invited his old enemy to have supper with the family. Morgan entertained the family with tales of his travels, and after supper asked the little boy if he would go fire hunting with him that night, offering to pay the boy a whole dollar for his help. The little boy, called Jimmy after his father, agreed eagerly, and they left right after supper.

Hours passed, and Jimmy's parents grew worried when he didn't return by bedtime. The hermit went in one direction and his wife in another, searching for their little boy. The hermit found no sign of the hunters, so he turned back the way he'd come. At daybreak he stumbled across the body of his wife, lying stiff and silent on the ground. She was unconscious and barely breathing. One side of her face had collapsed as if she had suffered a stroke of some kind. The hermit carried her back to this very clearing where we now sat and found that their cabin had been burned to the ground while they were gone. The hermit was furious. Morgan must have done this. But why? And where was little Jimmy?

He eased his wife to the ground and tended her as best he could, wondering what he should do. He couldn't leave her, but he had to find little Jimmy. Unless, he thought, his heart gripped with terror, little Jimmy had been in the house when it burned!

Then his wife stirred and opened her eyes. They were wide with horror. In a slurred, mumbling voice quite unlike her own, she told her husband what had happened to her. She had been searching for Jimmy when she saw him with the man Morgan in a boat down by the river. True to his pirate heritage, Morgan had long been stealing gold from the settlers. He had taken little Jimmy down to the hidden boat on the riverbank to help him bury his ill-gotten gains.

She hadn't known what to do. If the pirate knew she had seen his chest of treasure, he might kill both her and Jimmy to ensure their silence. But if she kept hidden, there was a good chance he would spare Jimmy, trusting that his parents would consider any tales he told of treasure to be the fanciful stories of the young. So she hid behind the palm trees and watched as the boy and the pirate lifted a heavy chest full of treasure from the boat, dug a deep hole in the bank, and placed the chest inside it. Jimmy was stooping over, securing the chest inside the hole, when Morgan suddenly stabbed him in the back with a dagger and pushed the dead boy into the hole with the treasure chest.

She opened her mouth to scream, ready to fling herself at the murdering pirate and avenge her boy. But at that moment, pain had pierced through her skull and she had fallen to the ground where her husband had found her, unable to move. She could see Morgan filling in the hole and concealing it with brush, but neither her voice nor her body would respond to her will. She was forced to observe the burying of the treasure chest and her son without being able to do anything to avenge the death of her little boy. When he was done, Morgan had walked right past her in the darkness without seeing her, heading back toward their cabin.

The hermit listened carefully to his wife's story. It was hard to make out all the words, for her tongue was partially paralyzed from her stroke, but he learned enough to make him turn pale with rage. He wanted to leap up and run after the murdering Morgan. He wanted to avenge his son. But he couldn't leave his wife. His arms tightened around her as she finished her story. She was silent for a moment, and then a sudden spasm caused her body to flail about. A moment later, she was dead.

The hermit cradled his wife to his chest and stared at the ashes of their once-happy home. Morgan must have torched the house, thinking they were inside, so that they would not come looking for their missing boy, he thought dully as he rocked his wife's body back and forth as though she were a tiny baby. Morgan was long-gone by now, but he would return someday for his treasure. And he—the hermit—would be waiting for him.

There was a long silence after the hermit finished his story.

"And you started wearing the gingham dress and sunbonnet because?" I asked at last.

"Because I wanted to be close to my wife," said the hermit. "And because my other clothes wore out and I had no money to buy more. Now I'm afraid it's become a habit!" The old man grinned at me from underneath the sunbonnet as he said the last words. At that moment, I caught a glimpse of the fellow he must have been before his wife and son died. A fellow who was a lot like my dead papa.

I didn't see the hermit for almost two months after that. I was back in school, and Mama kept me busy with chores over the weekend. I was sweeping the back porch one Saturday when Mama called to me from the sitting room to tell me I had company. The hermit was standing on the front porch with his sunbonnet in his hand, chatting awkwardly with Mama when I arrived at a run. We sat down on the steps, and Mama fetched us some cookies and lemonade and then left us alone together, since it was obvious that her company made the old man nervous.

After a few minutes of munching, the hermit said, "He come, Emma. He come at long last."

"You mean Morgan?" I breathed.

The hermit nodded. Then he told me what happened.

The hermit had been watching the banks of the river for three times as many years as I'd been alive and was afeard he would die before Morgan came back for his treasure. Then, two days ago, he saw a man digging a hole underneath a stout pine tree near the river and recognized the pirate that had murdered his little boy. As the hermit approached, the pirate threw a bone out of the hole he was digging. It was a child's arm bone. It fell at the hermit's feet, and the old man had given a wordless shout of sheer rage at the sight of it. Morgan dropped his shovel and cowered back as the hermit in his torn dress with the snakeskin belt and sunbonnet towered over him like the wrath of God.

"What in God's name are you?" Morgan gasped in horror.

"Don't you call on God!" the hermit roared. "You are a thief and a murderer. It is the Devil you should call on, for you are going to hell for your evil deeds."

"Who are you?" Morgan cried once again.

"I'm Jim Baines," the hermit howled. "And you killed my son!"

He leapt upon the old pirate, lifting him right over his head and running like a mad-thing through the forest with him until he reached the clearing where his strange cabin stood, where his dead wife lay buried, where Devil lurked in his pool.

"Go to the Devil!" the hermit screamed, and threw the murdering pirate into the open jaws of his monstrous alligator.

I gasped. "Is he? Is he?" I asked, unable to finish my question.

"He's dead. I think he gave Devil a stomachache," said the old man.

We sat for a long time, watching the sun set over the trees. I didn't blame the hermit one bit. The pirate had murdered his family and deserved what he got. That was as far as I'd got in my thinking when the hermit stirred and reached into the pocket of the worn blue-gingham dress. He pulled out a bit of paper and handed it to me.

"You hold onto that, Emma," he said. "The directions to the buried chest are on that paper. Someday you'll have a beau and want to get married. That money will give you a start."

I stared at the paper in my hand. "But Mr. Baines, that money belongs to you. You deserve it after what that man did to you and yours."

129

The hermit shook his head. "I want you to have it. I'm an old man. I don't need it. You're the nearest thing I got to kinfolk, and I want to make sure yer provided fer."

He patted my hand and rose abruptly. He nodded to me once, lifted a hand to Mama, who had appeared in the doorway, and strolled off into the rays of the setting sun.

A week later, a small carving of an alligator appeared on our porch with a note that said, "Take good care of Devil. He will miss me when I am gone." The words were followed by a series of hand signals that Devil responded to.

I studied the hand signals for a few minutes. Then I put the note in my pocket and went out back to look in our duck pond. All the ducks were huddled at the far end of the pond. At the near end, a huge pair of eyes peered at me from the murky depths.

"Good morning, Devil," I said. The big alligator surfaced for a moment and splashed his tail in greeting, the way the hermit had taught him. Mama wasn't going to be too pleased to have a giant alligator living in our duck pond, I thought. On the other hand, we weren't going to be bothered by tramps or wanderers ever again.

"It's a good thing I made an extra chicken pie for supper," I said to Devil. I made a small gesture with my hand and watched the big alligator nod his head enthusiastically, just as if he understood me.

At the edge of the clearing, I saw a flash of blue-gingham and the wave of the hermit's wrinkled hand. Then he was gone. I never saw the hermit again.

19

Spook Hill

LAKE WALES

He was a good chief and a wise man. So when, one by one, people began to go missing at night from their village, his first thought was *rogue alligator.* While others were murmuring of evil spirits, Cufcowellax was watching the lake. There were several large alligators in residence. It might be one of them. But Cufcowellax did not think so. One of the missing villagers had been a grown man—a strong warrior who would have put up quite a fight against any man or beast who threatened him. Yet no one had seen him taken, and there had been no tracks on the ground near his home. Just a trace of blood among his blankets indicated the fate he had suffered during the dark hours of the night.

Cufcowellax gathered the men together and laid a trap for the massive alligator, one that had worked before when a large bull got out of hand. Cufcowellax and his people slept a little easier that night, knowing the trap was there. But the trap was empty in the morning, and a child had disappeared from her home during the night, leaving just a trace of blood behind on her covers. Cufcowellax was furious. This had to stop. He was sure it was a clever alligator, but he needed to know more.

That morning, Cufcowellax paddled out onto the lake and found a concealed place among the tall reeds. Then he waited and watched. He watched white egrets fishing. He watched bullfrogs catching flies. He watched fish swimming. And he watched as two large alligators grew nervous and then swam away to the far end of the lake.

To his right, the huge bumpy log lying in the muddy water opened its eyes and crept slowly toward his canoe. It was a mammoth bull alligator. Cufcowellax had never seen an alligator so large. He estimated that it was nearly eighteen feet in length, and it amazed him that such a giant gator could have gone undetected for so many weeks.

And then it looked him in the eye, and Cufcowellax knew that this was no common alligator. This was an evil spirit that had taken the form of a gator, and it was preying upon his people, one by one. He grabbed his paddle and hurried out of the reed bed as fast as possible, before the huge beast rammed into him. *This is not going to be easy,* he thought as he paddled back across the lake to the village.

Cufcowellax gathered the men and told them what he had seen. Together the men set off onto the lake armed with spears to find and kill the huge bull alligator. It evaded them. It was astonishing. One moment they would see it right in front of them—the next moment a large figure would be on the opposite shore. The men grew fearful, and finally their chief ordered them to turn back for the village. Just before they reached it, a huge head appeared out of the water and coughed impudently into Cufcowellax's face. The bull alligator disappeared underwater with barely a ripple.

That cough infuriated the wise chief. He spoke at length with the tribe's religious leaders that evening, and for the next three days he underwent a special ceremony to put him under the protection of the Great Spirit. On the fourth evening, he sat in a hidden place near the edge of the water, armed only with a knife. He waited in silence for the coming of darkness, for the coming of the alligator.

Darkness fell suddenly, and with it came a cool breeze. The stars twinkled overhead, and around him the world grew still and silent. For a long time, Cufcowellax waited, listening to the small sounds of night creatures feeding, of the wind rustling in the tall grass. Then the sounds of the creatures faded into silence—a menacing silence pierced only by the wind in the trees. Cufcowellax felt every muscle in his body tense as his ears strained to hear a noise, any sound that might betray the whereabouts of the evil bull alligator. He heard nothing. It was coming on to dawn. Surely the creature must be in the village by now. It could not get passed without him seeing it. Could it? Perhaps the evil spirit within it was masking it even now from his sight!

Then Cufcowellax heard the faintest of slithering sounds in the grass only two yards away from his hiding place. Shivers ran up and down his arms, and his hand gripped reflexively on the handle of his knife. Breathing a prayer to the Great Spirit, he leapt forward in the dim grayness that preceded the dawn. He landed on the back of a huge bull alligator that was dragging the body of a dead village woman down to the lake. The gator gave a grunt of surprise and dropped the woman. Cufcowellax gave a great shout and wrapped his arms quickly around the gator's muzzle so that it couldn't bite him.

And then they were thrashing all over the shore of the lake, rolling over and over again. The gator tried to rip the Seminole chief with his claws, tried to beat him to death with his huge tail,

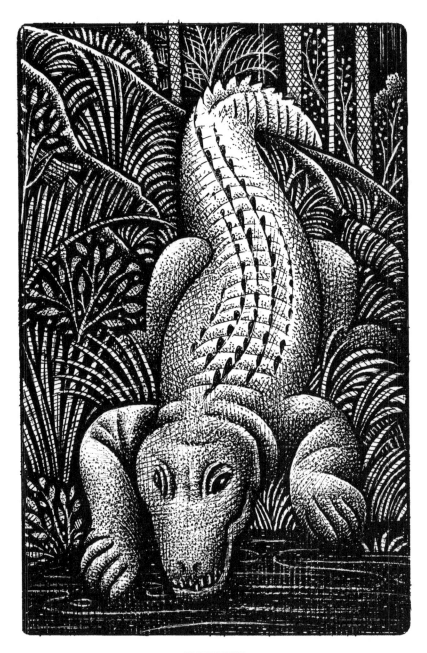

SPOOK HILL

tried to rub him off against the hard ground. Cufcowellax held on grimly, stabbing his knife into the underbelly of the huge bull alligator whenever he could get a hand free, which was not often. Dust whirled up around them as their thrashing bodies dug deeper and deeper into the bank. They made a huge hole in the ground as they thrashed and wrestled. Neither man nor alligator could gain the upper hand. Cufcowellax was hampered by the need to keep the huge gator's mouth shut, and the gator couldn't get Cufcowellax off his body long enough to kill him. Its clawed feet ripped at the chief's clothes, scoring his back and shoulders. Cufcowellax hung on grimly as the lake water began pouring into the huge hole they'd dug into the shore.

They were both covered in mud and thrashing about wildly when the bull alligator gave a huge thrust of its tail and managed to right itself. The gator slid the last few feet down into the water of the lake, with Cufcowellax clinging grimly to its back. The villagers, summoned by the tremendous noise of the fight, watched in horror as their chief disappeared beneath the dark water.

But a tremendous splashing and churning in the water indicated that the fight was not over. Cufcowellax surfaced, holding the end of a long tail, and took a huge gasping breath of air. Then he disappeared again, and the thrashing continued underwater, stirring up so much mud that no one could see what was going on.

Then, as suddenly as it started, the thrashing ceased. The water calmed and grew red with blood. The chief's wife moaned and fell to her knees, and their grown son gripped his mother's shoulder, his own face pale with fear.

All at once, Cufcowellax burst forth from the water with a tremendous splashing that soaked the villagers standing on the edge of the lake. He was bloodied and battered—but very much alive. He staggered as he strode from the lake, dragging the huge body of the evil bull alligator behind him. As soon as they were both free of the water, he collapsed onto his knees and fell into the arms of his wife and son.

As the story was told in later years, the Great Spirit had given Cufcowellax extraordinary strength and the ability to go for long periods underwater without breathing. It was these two advantages that had finally defeated the evil alligator spirit and saved the village.

Water continued to seep into the huge depression created during the fight between the chief and the bull alligator until it formed a second, smaller lake beside the first one. When Cufcowellax died a short time after the fight, having never fully recovered from his injuries, he was buried on the shore of the smaller lake.

From that time forward, circuit riders and other visitors to the area found that, against the laws of nature, the gradual slope leading down toward the lake was much more difficult to traverse than the climb up the other side. On the downward slope, horses strained against an invisible force that tried to push them back up the hill. It was unnerving. Travelers began calling the place Spook Hill and claimed that the strange phenomenon was caused by the evil spirit of the bull alligator seeking revenge against all who passed that way. Others said it was the spirit of the great chief Cufcowellax, eternally reliving his fight with the alligator.

Whatever the cause, the downhill slope continued to be a struggle for pioneers driving their wagons along the old army trail. Later, when the road was paved over, children riding their bikes to school found the downhill slope much more difficult to navigate than the uphill one. And to this day, if you put your car in neutral on Spook Hill, it will seem to travel backward up the hill, as if the evil spirit of the bull alligator is pushing it out of the way.

20

Pink

DAYTONA BEACH

She was always in the garden—day after day after day. It drove him crazy. Every waking hour was spent in the garden, which meant that supper never came when he wanted it and he had to go outside and kneel down in the dirt every dad-blamed time he wanted to have a conversation with his wife.

When he complained, she told him to get his own supper, even though she knew he was so bad at cooking that he could burn a pot of boiling water. "So get some pizza," she said. He didn't like pizza, he told her. "Tough luck," she said, and kept working in her garden.

The garden wasn't the only thing that drove him crazy. His wife also loved the color pink. She wore something pink every dad-blamed day of her life, and most of the flowers in the garden were pink—pink phlox, pink daisies, pink peonies, and pink roses. "Choose another color," he yelled one day when the overwhelming pinkness of the garden made his head ache. So what color did she choose? Mauve!

"Mauve is just pink in disguise," he grumbled, and his wife laughed at him. She had an infectious laugh, and after frowning for a moment longer, he laughed too. Overall, his wife was a great lady to have around, and he'd marry her again in an instant. She had a great deal of charm, and she cooked divinely when she had a mind to cook. The house was always clean and neat, if a little too pink on the interior for his tastes, and their garden really was a showplace. She put up with his funny little ways, keeping the medicine cabinet in precisely the order he liked it and making sure he had fresh cantaloupe every day for breakfast. At least she couldn't turn that pink, he conceded—even if she did serve it on a plate rimmed with pink roses.

They were getting on a bit in years when his wife started complaining about her knees. She had some arthritis in them, and kneeling was difficult. She wanted an assistant to help her in the garden during the afternoons. "Why do you need an assistant?" he grumbled. "Do *you* want to help me?" she retorted. "Heck no," he replied, and told her to go ahead and hire a gardener.

He didn't expect the handsome young fellow who showed up the next day to help his still-attractive wife in the garden. The fellow was well set up too, with plenty of muscle and a charming manner that soon had his wife laughing and fluffing up her hair as they talked among the flowers. That drove him really crazy. She never fluffed her hair for him, dad blame it! His wife, for all her arthritis, was still fairly young and good-looking to boot. Some folks might think it was natural for her to find the new gardener charming. There was nothing in it, they might say. But he wondered. Oh how he wondered.

He started coming home early from work to spy on his wife and the new gardener. They were always talking and laughing together as they worked. He didn't like it. Then his wife went out and bought a brand-new red lipstick, though she'd only ever bought pink lipstick before. That really made him suspicious. And she went out and got her hair cut in a new style that made her look years younger. That made him hopping mad. Something was up between her and the gardener. He knew it! But he could never catch them doing anything but digging and planting and weeding in the garden. It drove him crazy.

Finally he confronted the new gardener in the driveway one afternoon while his wife was out buying seedlings at the garden center. The young man denied that there was any hanky-panky going on between himself and his female employer, but her husband knew better and fired the gardener on the spot. When his wife returned, he told her the gardener had gone home ill, and she believed him.

During dinner that evening, he confronted his wife with his suspicions. "I'm not having an affair," she retorted when she realized the direction his questions were taking. "But if you keep this up, he could get lucky." Her smart reply filled him with rage. A red-hot mist filling his eyes, he grabbed blindly for his wife and started shaking her, his hands closing around her neck. It was several minutes before he calmed down enough to realize he was shaking a limp rag-doll figure that was no longer breathing. It took another moment to drop his wife's dead body on the floor in horror, realizing what he'd done—and what would happen to him if he got caught.

Fortunately for him, the ground was always disturbed around his house because of his wife's incessant gardening. He just needed to stir up the latest patch, dump his wife's body underneath it, and cover the grave-mound with the pink flower seedlings his wife had just brought back from the garden center. End of problem.

Pink

He closed the house the next day, telling their friends and neighbors that they were going North to be near his wife's ailing sister. Then he went far away from the house among the pink flowers and tried to forget. A few years later he sold the house to a young couple, who seemed delighted by the neglected garden and paid his asking price without any dickering.

When seven years had passed without suspicion from the authorities, he decided it was safe to come home. He got an apartment in town and settled down to resume some of his old friendships and activities. Anyone who asked was told that his wife had left him some time ago and he didn't like to talk about it. Respecting his wishes, his acquaintances never brought up the subject.

But he realized one day that he was still frightened of discovery. He had to know if his wife was still buried in the garden. He started watching his old house, waiting for the young couple to leave so he could check the hidden grave. When the young couple left for the weekend, he slipped into the garden at dusk and hurried quietly to the place where he had buried his wife. To his shock and horror, he saw that the old grave-mound was still planted with pink flowers—and those flowers formed the shape of a woman! His hands were shaking as he prodded the soil with a spade. He dug a deep, narrow hole, poking down carefully to feel for his wife's bones, but he found nothing. He dug deeper, widening the hole in panic. Still nothing. Her body was gone!

Alarmed, he made discreet inquiries around the neighborhood the next day, speaking only to people who had never met either himself or his wife. One of them told him that the young couple had found a family gravesite on the property and had the

PINK

grave moved to the local cemetery, since they did not wish to maintain the grave at their own expense. He felt a surge of relief at this explanation, but morbid curiosity sent him along to the cemetery to check on the truth of the tale.

He walked around for a long time, searching for a grave with no name. Perhaps it had no stone either. He could not be sure. Then he caught a glimmer of pink, and the pulse started pounding painfully in his wrists and neck. Could it be? He walked toward the place, his left arm tingling painfully. Yes, there was a narrow grave with no name attached to it, covered with pink flowers. It was his wife. He knew it was.

In that moment, the red mist rose once again before his eyes. The tingling in his left arm became a sharp pain, and he felt his body arch in agony before he tumbled down among the pink flowers. The whole world went dark, and his last thought was of the rag-doll figure in his hands that had once been his happy wife.

A caretaker found his dead body later that evening. When the authorities removed it, the pink flowers he had crushed in his fall never grew back on the unmarked grave.

To this day, there is still a body-size swath cut through the pink flowers that grow across the unmarked grave. And in the old house where the couple once lived, the pink flowers on the empty grave mound still grow each spring in the shape of a woman's body, no matter how many times the owners have uprooted them and planted something else in their place.

21

Spanish Moss

THE FLORIDA COAST

It was early fall when the captain and his men made camp on the coast, planning to hunt and fish for a week to supplement their meager supplies with fresh meat. Their regiment was charged with exploring and taming the wilds of this new land they had discovered, and they planned to march northward for many days.

Among the company was a beautiful Native American woman they had captured during a skirmish a few days previous. The Spanish soldiers had killed all their native attackers but had spared the life of the woman and had brought her along with them. In truth, they might have let her go had the captain not been smitten by her. She was tall and graceful, with masses of long dark hair and luminous dark eyes. He had never seen her equal for loveliness or spirit.

The captain tried to woo the beautiful captive as they journeyed northward, inviting her to dine in his tent, picking wildflowers for her, and reciting Spanish poetry to her. But the lovely captive spurned his advances and demanded that he release her so that she might return to her people. As his hopes of winning her love evaporated, the captain's infatuation turned

to hatred. He was furious at the woman's open defiance, afraid
that it might undermine his standing among the troops.

The situation came to a head that evening. The woman was
stirring the fire, and a long strand of her silky hair fell across her
cheek. When the captain reached out and brushed it gently back
behind her ear, the woman slapped his face, right in front of his
men. Enraged, the captain struck her a fierce blow, sending her
flying backward into the dirt. Leaping to his feet, he towered
over the beautiful captive and swore he would cut off her head
and put it on a pike by the entrance to his camp as a warning to
any who defied him.

The woman raised her chin defiantly and said, "If you do this
evil deed, I swear my spirit will follow you wherever you go!"

With an incoherent shout of rage, the captain drew his
sword and slashed downward three times. The third cut severed
the woman's head from her neck. Grabbing the head by its
silky black hair, the captain strode to the edge of camp, blood
dripping in his wake. He thrust a pike through the bottom of
the head and buried the end of the pike in the ground so that
the head could be seen by all his men. The woman's face was
set in a look of defiance, even in death, and her long, silky hair
twisted this way and that in the breeze. The captain marched
back to his tent and got very drunk, and the men avoided him
for the rest of the evening.

But in the morning, one of the officers came hurrying
into the tent, his cheeks pale with fright. "Sir, the head . . .
the woman . . . " he stuttered incoherently, unable to finish a
sentence. The captain waved for him to continue, but he just
beckoned mutely to his superior officer to follow him outside.
As soon as he stepped foot out of the tent, the captain could

see what had frightened the man. The woman's head atop the bloodstained pike was now standing right outside his tent. Overnight her long black hair had turned gray; her face was pointed directly toward his tent, her defiant dead eyes fixed upon its entrance.

The captain's heart thundered within him at the sight. "Is this someone's idea of a joke?" he roared, using anger to hide his fear.

"No, sir," the officer babbled. "The men swear that they did not touch it. They say it is the curse come true."

"I don't believe in curses," the captain snapped, cold sweat running down his back, despite his words. "Put the head back at the entrance to the camp, and tell the men that the first one who touches it will be severely punished!"

The captain stormed back into his tent. It was only when he was alone that he staggered into a chair, his knees trembling too much to keep him upright. What had he done?

During breakfast, his eyes moved more than once to the bloodstained pike at the entrance to the camp. As he finished his meal and rose to his feet, the pike suddenly vanished. The captain gasped and hurried forward, one step, two. He almost rammed into the head on the pike, which reappeared right in front of him, the woman's eyes gazing defiantly into his own, her long gray hair blowing wildly about the bloodstained pike, even though no wind was blowing. The captain screamed in terror, staggering backward with his hands in front of his face. He babbled a prayer aloud as his men came running. At the sight of the ghastly head on the pike, they retreated behind their captain.

"Take it down," the captain roared. "Take it down and bury it! Now!"

After a palpable hesitation, a few of the braver officers came forward to deal with the head on the pike. When it was gone, the captain staggered back into his tent and fell on his knees, vomiting his breakfast onto the ground. Mother of God, what was happening to him?

Taking long, slow breaths, the captain reminded himself that the woman was dead and that the curse of a native could not prevail over a good Catholic like himself. Could it?

He had cleaned himself up and donned a new uniform by the time his officers came to report that the head was buried deep beneath a stone. He nodded his thanks and started giving out the day's orders as if nothing had happened. And nothing did happen for the rest of the day. As they realized the haunting— or whatever it was—had ceased, the activity around the camp grew cheerful. They had foiled the curse of the native woman! She was dead and buried and would haunt them no longer. The captain went to sleep in good spirits. They would stay here for a week, he decided, before making their way northward. It would do the men good to have a rest.

He was awakened the next morning by a man's scream coming from the edge of camp. He was up and armed as soon as his eyes opened, prepared for an attack by the area natives. He ran outside and joined the other men racing toward the sound, swords drawn. At the edge of camp they found an officer shivering from head to toe. When he saw his comrades in various stages of dress waving their swords, he pointed to the tree beneath which the woman's head had been buried. Hanging from the tree were long, silky gray strands blowing in the sea breeze. The captain gasped, shivers running up his arms and spine. It was her hair! The woman's hair!

Then the man nearest the officer, who was a bit of a daredevil, stepped forward and grabbed the hair off the tree. "It's moss, you fool!" he said. "Just moss!"

Just moss, the captain repeated to himself. But it was unlike any moss he had ever seen before—not on this island, not in Florida, not anywhere in the Spanish empire. And it looked just like her hair . . .

"I've had enough of this nonsense," the captain said aloud. "Break camp. We're heading north!"

"Yes, sir," his men replied. With many a backward glance toward the moss now lying on the ground, the soldiers hurried away to do as he ordered. When they were gone, the captain buried the moss in the earth under the tree. They would leave this cursed place and travel north to fulfill their mission.

The captain didn't relax until they had marched many miles to the north. Just to be safe, he inspected the trees around the clearing where they made camp that night. There was no sign of any long-haired moss growing upon them. Good.

The captain slept soundly that night, undisturbed by the rising wind that came in from the sea. He was the first one up in the morning. As he stepped out into the grove of trees, his eyes were caught by long, gray strands growing from every branch. The trees were covered with hair! *No, not hair, moss,* he corrected himself. But he remembered the native woman's curse: "If you do this evil deed, I swear my spirit will follow you wherever you go!" And the moss had followed him up the coast. He stood frozen to the spot as his men awakened around him. One by one, they came to stare at the moss-trimmed trees. The moss blew frantically back and forth in a breeze they could not feel. And the captain could sense the dead woman's gaze upon him, though her head was buried far away.

"Let's go," he snapped, finally breaking the uncanny silence. Without a word, his men broke camp, and they hurried away without pausing to eat. The captain could feel the eyes of his men on his back as they marched, though none dared speak of what they had seen.

They paused at midday to break their fast. While they ate, the captain could see the bare trees growing moss. It slithered down the trunks and slid up and over branches, gray and silky and waving in a nonexistent breeze. The troop hurried through their meal and almost ran out of the clearing. As they marched northward, the moss followed them. The few times he glanced over his shoulder, the captain saw moss growing over the bare trees in their wake. He felt sick to his stomach, and it was only the force of his iron will that kept his meal down.

Grimly they continued their journey. A breeze sprang up from the sea, and on the breeze was a familiar voice—a woman's voice. "I will follow you," it whispered in the captain's ear. "I will follow you."

They only stopped marching when sheer darkness forced them to pause. They camped on the beach well away from the trees, and the men built a huge bonfire. Only the captain's tent was erected that night, and he went into it reluctantly, still hearing a voice on the breeze. Or was it only in his head?

When the captain did not emerge from his tent the next morning, the officers went inside to check on him. His bed was rumpled but empty. Alarmed, they hurried outside and began searching the beach for their commander. And then they saw a figure dangling from a gnarled oak at the edge of the beach.

SPANISH MOSS

The men hurried toward it and saw their captain hanging by the neck from a thickly tangled skein of gray moss. The moss had strangled the life out of him and was growing all over his dangling body.

The men stared at the moss-covered figure in terror. Finally the daredevil soldier cut him down. The officers ordered camp broken down, and the troop retreated south toward St. Augustine, abandoning all pretext of obeying orders now that their commander was dead. They stayed as close to the shore as they could, trying to avoid the trees. The moss followed them.

When the company broke up in St. Augustine, the soldiers were reassigned to other units and sent many places around the world. Wherever a soldier from that ill-fated unit journeyed, the moss followed him. In time the newly christened "Spanish" moss covered the whole South. Today it is seen in many places around the world; a silent witness to injustice revenged.

22

Mystic Music

MANATEE COUNTY

I am old now, and my life draws to its close. Many are the memories that have fled from my aged mind. But even in the winter of my lifetime, one story burns brightly in the darkness that draws me slowly into its embrace. The youngest of our tribe will never remember the ship that came so long ago. But they hear the mystic music when the mist rises off the river, and they wonder. Some of them remember the old storyteller who sits quietly in the corner, eating soft food because his teeth are all gone. And they come and ask me to tell them the old story again. This I do gladly so that the tale may not be lost to future generations.

I was medicine man then, in the prime of my life with my children nearly grown and my wife still strong and beautiful at my side. We still courted like young ones, my wife and I, and we were courting each other one spring night, cuddling together on the bank of the river, when we heard shouting in the distance and the slap of waves against a massive hull. Startled, we drew apart and hurried to a clear place along the river to see what was happening.

From our new vantage point, our eyes beheld an amazing sight. A huge canoe—the like of which we had never seen—was coming rapidly up the river against the current. At first I thought it had wings, like a huge bird. But as it drew closer I realized that the wings were actually large cloths hanging from poles. I surmised that the cloths were meant to catch the wind and make the canoe go very fast. At the front of the canoe was the head of a fierce creature with claws, scales, and large teeth. It reminded me of an alligator with wings. The canoe was lit by torches, and in their light we saw white-skinned, yellow-haired men working the ropes controlling the "wings." They were working frantically, obviously terrified of something behind them. Their fear was palpable. It made my stomach tighten, and I groped for the knife I was not wearing.

My wife and I clung together in the shadow of the trees, wondering who these white-skinned strangers were and where they were going. Then we heard shouting from downriver and saw, at a distance, that two more large canoes were following the first. I had been in enough battles to know when an enemy means to destroy the one they chase, and I easily read that menace in the approaching boats. No wonder the white-skinned ones were so afraid.

Aboard the huge canoe before us there was much frantic activity. The white-skinned men were hauling strange pack-ages up to the edge of the canoe and throwing them over the side. As they did, a woman appeared at the front of the huge canoe, beside the carved beast like a flying alligator. She held a strange, stringed object in her hands, and she began to play it while the men aboard the canoe tossed their packages into the river's dark waters. Music floated over the water. It was so lovely that my wife started to cry. The woman with the musical instrument had long hair that rippled to her waist. It was as golden as the rising sun. I had never before seen such hair.

The huge canoe before us seemed to lurch in the water as the woman played, and I realized with a sudden jerk of my heart that it was rapidly sinking into the river. The craft was so deep in the water that the slight wind filling the cloths could no longer move it. Water poured in over the sides of the canoe, washing the feet of the warriors and the lovely woman playing the music.

"We must save them," my wife whispered. Her words were echoed by several voices from behind us, and we realized that the shouts of the men in the pursuing canoes had summoned others from our village.

Suddenly there was a flare of brilliant light and a huge boom like thunder. It came from one of the enemy boats pursuing the yellow-haired ones. Something huge and round smashed into the part of the large canoe that was still above the water. The canoe broke apart before our eyes, throwing the yellow-haired men and the lovely musical woman into the water. With astonishing speed, the ailing canoe disappeared beneath the dark water of the river, the large poles with their cloths falling into the river like logs and sinking along with the rest. What was more terrible than the sinking of the canoe was the absolute silence that followed it. The woman's haunting music had ceased abruptly in the violence of the blast.

The wind sprang up around us as we stood frozen, stunned by what had just happened. The enemy canoes were suddenly upon us, sailing right over the place where the canoe of the yellow-haired people had sunk moments before. The dark-skinned men in their winged canoes had angry faces and menacing eyes. At the sight of them, I motioned for our

people to fall back into the trees. Anyone who could make such a large boom and sink a huge canoe like the one we'd seen was not to be trifled with. There was nothing we could do for the strange white-skinned people. They had gone to their death bravely and in silence, save for the sound of the woman's music. Whatever was in the packages they had thrown overboard was now amply guarded by their spirits, and I for one would never betray their treasure to those evil men who had murdered them with one blinding blast.

The enemy disappeared up the river, angrily searching for the canoe they had unknowingly sunk in the night. They never found it. And they never found us, for I ordered our people to remain in the village, save for a few warriors who watched the river until the enemy had turned their winged canoes and gone back out to the bay.

The story was repeated with wonder among our people, and a few of the younger boys wanted to dive down and get the packages thrown into the river by the yellow-haired men. But we forbade them to do so. The men had died to preserve those packages, and their spirits would remain to protect them. To take them from the river would anger the spirits and be a terrible act of sacrilege against the beautiful woman who had played her mystic music as they died.

I dreamt about that haunting music more than once during the year that followed. Would I ever hear such a wonderful sound again? I even tried to make an instrument like the one the yellow-haired woman played, but it squawked at me sourly. My wife finally burned it because it was making her crazy with its terrible noise.

A year after the chase of the winged canoes, as the youngsters in the village had dubbed the story, I was awakened by the

MYSTIC MUSIC

lovely sound of a stringed instrument. It was playing a tune I recognized immediately as the song played by the yellow-haired woman. My wife had awakened before me and lay listening to the music. We rose together and followed the sound down to the Manatee River. The sound came from the center of the river, directly over the place where the winged ship had sunk the previous year. We stood hand in hand, listening to the music as other members of our tribe crowded on the bank beside us. This time the song played all the way to the end, untroubled by the enemy blast that had interrupted it a year ago. We didn't see the spirit of the yellow-haired maiden, but we knew she was there, guarding the treasure buried at the bottom of the river.

Ever after, the mystical music sounded on the Manatee River once every year in the spring. We looked forward to it, my wife and I, and whenever we heard it, we told the story to our children and our grandchildren.

I am old now and have heard the mystic music many times. It is my hope that I will live until spring so that I may hear it once more before death closes my eyes. And who knows? Perhaps, when the Great Spirit calls me home, it will be to the sound of a mystic stringed instrument playing my favorite song.

23

The Choking Doberman

TAMPA

After a bad day at work, I was relieved to pull into my driveway and park the car in the garage. *Thank God it is Friday,* I thought as I grabbed my handbag from the passenger seat. I headed through the kitchen door, already planning what I would make for my daughter and myself for dinner. My husband was away on a business trip, so it was just the two of us this weekend.

I was pulling things out of the refrigerator when I heard a funny grunting sound coming from the living room. That was strange. I put a head of lettuce down by the sink and went into the living room, trying to track down the sound. Could it be Lenny, our Doberman pinscher? Now that I thought about it, it was strange that he hadn't met me at the door. I heard the funny coughing sound again. It sounded like Lenny was choking. But where was he? I hunted behind the couch, under the piano. He wasn't there. I finally found him in the hallway near the closet, crouched on the floor, trying desperately to breathe against something lodged in his throat.

I dropped to my knees beside him, terrified. Lenny was choking! What should I do? I wasn't sure how one did the Heimlich maneuver on a dog, but I tried it anyway. Lenny kept choking. I tried reaching down his throat, but the object was too deep for me to reach it.

By this time I was frantic. If I left him like this, our beloved pet would die. But my daughter's bus was due home in half an hour, and with my husband away, there was no one to meet her. My mother was in a nursing home, my sister was overseas, and our neighbors didn't get home until after six.

Grimly, I lifted our heavy dog and carried him through the kitchen into the garage. I laid him on the front seat of the car, stroking his ears and telling him to hang on. Then I drove to the vet's, breaking every speed limit along the way. I rushed Lenny into the waiting room, shouting to the nurse that it was an emergency. She ran for the vet, who was luckily not with a patient. Together we got Lenny up onto the table. I explained as quickly as I could that my five-year-old was coming home on the bus and I needed to run home and pick her up.

"No problem. You go get your daughter," said the vet, already beginning his examination. "I'll call you when its time to pick up Lenny."

I was heartened by his attitude. *When* it was time to pick up Lenny, not *if.* I rubbed Lenny's ears one more time and left the office at a run. *Please, oh, please let me get home before the bus!*

It was a close thing, but I swung into the driveway three minutes before the bus was due. I just had time to get into the kitchen and put away the food I'd taken out of the refrigerator when the bus stopped at our driveway and my little girl came skipping in through the garage.

"Hi, Mom!" she called. "Can I have a snack?"

"Sure, honey," I said, pulling an apple out of the fruit bowl and cutting it into slices. I dropped a dollop of peanut

THE CHOKING DOBERMAN

butter on the plate and set it down in front of her while I told her about Lenny.

Her brown eyes widened in alarm. "Will he be all right, Mommy?" she asked anxiously.

"The veterinarian seemed to think so," I replied, sneaking an apple slice. "He's going to call us when Lenny is better."

As if sensing my words, the phone began ringing. "That's probably him now," I said, as much to reassure my daughter as myself. I picked up the phone and said hello into the receiver.

"Mrs. Johnson, is that you?" the veterinarian's voice sounded strange.

"Speaking," I said. "How is Lenny?"

"Mrs. Johnson, I need you to get your daughter and get out of your house right now," the veterinarian said in a tight voice.

"I beg your pardon?" I said, startled by his words.

"You've got to get out of the house right away," he repeated. "I just removed two human fingers from your dog's throat! I've already called the police."

I dropped the phone, lifted my little girl off her stool, ran out the garage door and down the driveway, and started jogging down the street. My daughter felt my fear and started to cry, not understanding what was wrong. To my relief, I saw a police car turning onto our street before I was halfway down the block. I waved it down and ran to the window. There were two officers inside. They looked like big, sturdy fellows who meant business, and I was reassured at the sight of them.

"Officer, I think there's someone in my house," I gasped. "My veterinarian just took two fingers out of my dog's throat."

The officer was already nodding his head. "Yes, ma'am, we just got the call. Where's your house?"

I pointed up the block and followed the police car back to our yard. The officer asked me to stay outside with my daughter, and I huddled on the garden bench, holding my little girl tight. After a moment, I heard one of the officers through the open window, exclaiming in surprise.

"I found him in the laundry room. He's unconscious."

A few minutes later, a second police car arrived, with an ambulance right behind it. They rolled the unconscious man past the garden bench on a gurney, and I got a good look at his right hand. It was covered in blood and missing two fingers.

When the police finished searching the house and declared it safe to reenter, I went to the phone and called a friend to come spent the night with my daughter and me. I didn't want to be alone. Then I called the veterinarian to thank him and ask about Lenny.

"Lenny's fine," the veterinarian said. "You can pick him up anytime."

We went immediately to pick up our dog, and I was thrilled to see Lenny back on his feet and happy to see us. I dropped to my knees and threw my arms around his neck.

"Good dog, Lenny," I said. "Good dog!"

24

The Witch's Curse

FORT LAUDERDALE

Once long ago, when the area that is now the city of Fort Lauderdale was just a small settlement, there lived a couple with eleven sons. The father was a poor farming man, so all those strapping boys came in right handy, helping him till the soil and make a profit. But the couple desperately wanted a little girl to balance things out a might. Someone to help her mama in the house, to climb trees and run races with her brothers, and to sit on her papa's knee when he told stories at nighttime. Even the boys thought a little sister would be a nice addition to their happy family. So they all started praying . . . and praying . . . and praying for the good Lord to send them a little girl. Nothing happened.

Now Madeleine, the boys' mama, was good friends with a local plantation owner's wife, and they often got together to drink tea at the lovely manor house where the rich woman lived. One afternoon, as they sat sewing on a quilt and sipping tea together, Madeleine confided her dream to the plantation owner's wife.

"I wish you had come to me sooner," her friend said earnestly, snipping off a spare thread with a small pair of scissors. "I would have sent you right down to old Granny Tucker's house in the village. She's a witch-woman, and I'm sure she could help you."

Madeleine pondered this as she carefully quilted a fern pattern onto the pink square in front of her. "I'm not sure my husband would like consulting a witch-woman," she said at last. "It rather smacks of black magic, and he's high church."

"Do you need to tell your husband?" asked her friend.

Madeleine nodded her head emphatically. "We tell each other everything," she said. "It's simpler that way."

"Well," said the rich lady, "I recommend Granny Tucker, if it's a little girl your after."

Madeleine thanked her friend and thought the matter through on the way home. She was uneasy consulting a witch, even a good one, but she longed to have a little girl. She had almost decided against the idea when the neighbor's daughter came skipping down the lane toward her, blond ringlets glowing in the dappled sunlight coming through the leaves of the palm trees overhead. Madeleine's heart caught in her throat and tears sprang to her eyes. Oh, to have a little girl like that! She smiled at the child through her tears, and then and there decided to speak to her husband about Granny Tucker.

Well the farmer hemmed and hawed a might when she brought up the witch. "I've heard she practices white magic during the day, but after dark it's all cursing and hexes and other nasty practices."

"I think this may be our last chance," Madeleine said quietly. "I'm getting too old for child-bearing."

Her husband flashed her a worried glance. He'd been thinking along those lines himself but hadn't wanted to say anything to his beloved wife. In Madeleine's face, he read hope and longing and sweet resignation. She was going to leave the matter up to him. This was against everything his religion said was right, but he could not deny his helpmate this one last hope. So the farmer consented.

The next day, after the work was done and the boys were in bed, the farmer and his wife slipped down to the village and knocked on Granny Tucker's door. The witch-woman opened the door immediately. For a moment she stood framed against the bright firelight, a stooped silhouette of utter darkness. Madeleine drew in a sharp breath, her heart thudding in sudden apprehension. Then the moment passed. Her eyes adjusted to the glare, and in the firelight she beheld a wrinkled old woman with crinkly white hair and a lined face. Her eyes were dark and sharp, and she leaned on a cane. Winding around the cane were shallowly incised symbols that seemed to writhe with their own energy. The handle of the cane was a snarling tiger's head. It was a thing of absolute evil, Madeleine knew instinctively, and she looked away from it at once, her thumbs pricking as all the tiny hairs on her arms stood on end. She wanted to run away. But she thought of the golden-haired neighbor girl, and so she stayed.

Her husband urged her inside with a hand under her elbow, and she passed the witch-woman in the doorway, being careful not to touch her. Old Granny Tucker chuckled as they went to stand before the fire, holding hands like a pair of nervous children.

"I see you coming, farmer-man, you and your wife there. You want something from Old Granny. A potion perhaps? There's a little girl in your fine lady's eyes that wants to be born but can't without some help."

As she spoke, the witch twisted her cane back and forth in her gnarled old hands. Her nails were long and filed to a point like claws. Madeleine shuddered to see them.

"We will pay you for the potion," her husband said bravely. "Whatever you want."

"It isn't paying I want. Not in money," said Granny Tucker. Madeleine's stomach lurched, and all the muscles in her back spasmed painfully, as if in warning.

"What is it you want?" she asked in a clear, high voice quite unlike her usual tone.

"I want your little girl," Granny Tucker said with a malicious smile. "The day she turns ten, I want her to come live with me and learn to conjure."

"I couldn't!" Madeleine protested. The very thought made her ill.

"No deal, no daughter," said the witch-woman. "Would you like to see her, the little girl stuck in your eyes?"

Her husband shook his head. "No, ma'am, we won't take up more of your time," he said. But Madeleine was struck by a longing so deep it bowed her in half. Hugging herself tightly, as if in pain, she whispered, "Yes."

Instantly, Granny Tucker waved her snarling-tiger cane in the air in front of them, and a white mist formed into a circle before their eyes. Inside the circle appeared the head and shoulders of a little girl with the farmer's eyes and Madeleine's oval face and enchanting smile. Her hair was black as midnight, her lips ruby red. Her skin was pale, but her cheeks were rosy, and her eyes sparkled with laughter.

"My baby," Madeleine gasped, feeling as if her heart would tear in two at the sight. "My baby."

Tears poured down her cheeks, and she felt her husband slip his arms around her. "All right," he said for them both, his voice husky with feeling. "We agree to your terms. Where is this potion of yours?"

Old Granny Tucker cackled in triumph and gestured to the rickety wood table in the center of the room. A thick brown bottle about six inches high materialized in the center. It was full of a dark liquid that filled the small room with a pungent smell.

"Drink it," she told Madeleine, "and remember your promise."

The smell nauseated her, and she knew she would have to drink the whole thing at once or she would not drink it at all. Bravely she grabbed the small bottle, tipped it up, and drank it down in one gulp. It tasted even worse than it smelled. She had to clap a hand over her mouth to keep from retching it up. Feeling queasy, she looked over at the witch, who was still standing near the door. "Is that all?"

"That's all," said Granny Tucker. She waved her cane at the door, which swung open of its own accord. Knowing they were dismissed, the farmer and his wife crept away, Madeleine very pale and queasy from the potion she'd taken.

And she remained pale and queasy every day for the next ten months. For the potion had done its job, and she conceived within a month after swallowing it down. The boys were delighted by the news and set to work with a will, building an addition onto the side of their house and kitting it out as a nursery. Everyone knew the baby would be a girl, even though Madeleine and her husband had never mentioned their trip to Granny Tucker's house.

Sylvia was born just before Christmas, and she was a perfect baby right from the start. She slept through the night by the end of the first month and whimpered politely when she was hungry or needed changing. She cooed in delight when she saw her brothers and cuddled up against her papa when he took her on his knee. She learned to sing as soon as she learned to talk, and she followed her mama all over, trying to help with the housework and care for the chickens and milk the cows. Her hair was black as midnight and curled in lovely ringlets down her back. Her white skin never freckled; neither did it tan in the sun, though she often forgot to wear her sunbonnet.

Sylvia was quick and smart, beautiful and funny. Everyone loved her—her parents, her brothers, neighbors, and people at church. The plantation owner's wife became her godmother and was as proud of Sylvia as if she were her own. After all, she was the one who'd advised her parents to go to Granny Tucker.

Madeleine and her husband avoided the old witch-woman whenever they could. The sight of her reminded them of promises they would rather forget. Madeleine was hoping the old woman would forget. Or perhaps she would pass before Sylvia turned ten. That last thought shamed her. It was terrible to wish for another's demise. She wouldn't do it, not even for her beloved child.

So Madeleine forced all thoughts of the promise to the witch-woman from her head and enjoyed the first nine years of Sylvia's young life with all the passionate love of a mother's heart. She made lovely dresses for her, gathered flowers with her, taught her to sew and quilt and embroider. She watched, laughing, as the boys taught her to play ball and climb trees and ride horses. She loved watching Sylvia racing around the paddock on top of a tall horse, her long black ringlets sailing out behind her. *My baby,* she thought. *My baby.*

As Sylvia's tenth birthday approached, Madeleine grew pale and sickly. Old Granny Tucker was still stumping around the village, and she cackled triumphantly whenever she caught sight of Sylvia. Madeleine knew the witch would come for her daughter. And what would she do then? Losing Sylvia would be like losing a limb. She would never get over the pain of it.

Her husband too was quiet and thoughtful. They carefully avoided talking of the matter, as if by not speaking of it they could make it go away. But neither of them were surprised when, a few minutes after dinner on Sylvia's tenth birthday, the door of their farmhouse blew open with a crash and Granny Tucker walked in, brandishing her snarling-tiger cane.

"I've come for the girl," she called. "Pack her things."

Sylvia gasped and shrank back in her chair. All eleven of her brothers, even the ones who were grown and married, were there to celebrate her birthday, and they leapt up as one and formed a protective line between Sylvia and the witch.

"No," the farmer thundered from his place at the head of the table. "You will not take my child!"

"Yes, I will," Granny Tucker shot back. "Remember your promise!"

Madeleine did remember their promise—and the way Granny Tucker had manipulated her longing to force the promise out of them. That wasn't right. Not right at all.

Madeleine stood tall and interposed herself between the witch and her children. All of them were precious to her, from her oldest son—more than a head taller than she and able to lift a wagon all on his own—to her little daughter. The witch could not have them!

"You can have none of our children," Madeleine said, thrusting out her chin defiantly. "Not one. You get out of here before I call the farm dogs!"

Old Granny Tucker's eyes flashed in fury. She raised her evil cane and gestured toward the windows. The glass shattered in them, one after the other, sending shards all over the room. Two of the boys grabbed their little sister and hustled her upstairs, while everyone else ducked under the table to avoid the flying glass. A foul-smelling wind poured through the jagged remains of the windows, making the farmer and his family gag. The witch threw back her head and laughed maniacally, waving her cane and shouting ancient words that burned the backs of their eyes and made their skin feel as though black sludge were pouring all over their bodies. From upstairs, Sylvia screamed and writhed in agony.

"No!" shouted Madeleine. "No!"

At her words, her eldest son and his brothers staggered forward against the terrible force of the wind and tackled the old witch, sending her sprawling backward through the door and down the steps to the ground. The wind ceased when she hit the dirt, and Sylvia stopped screaming in pain.

Shocked, the witch stared up at the huge farm boys standing over her, their arms crossed, faces grim and menacing. Glaring back she tried to rise. Immediately, Madeleine's eldest son picked her up as if she were a sack of potatoes, flung her over his shoulder, and marched toward the garden gate. The witch beat him on the back of his legs with her cane. He ignored the blows and stepped out into the road. Nine of his brothers followed along behind in three rows of three. The other boy remained behind to guard their parents and Sylvia.

"Where are you taking me?" shrieked the witch.

"I'm just seeing you home, ma'am," said Madeleine's eldest. "To make sure nothing happens to you along the way."

Old Granny Tucker let out a shriek of absolute rage. "You won't get away with this," she shouted in her piercing treble. "The girl will die! I'll make sure of that. She will die from a horse's hoof before the year is out!"

No one answered her. The boys just marched grimly onward in their lines of three, following their elder brother as he escorted the witch home. But Madeleine, standing on the front porch with her husband's arms around her, shuddered in terror. Could it be true? Could the witch curse her baby so that she died? New Year's Day was only a few days away . . .

"We'll keep her away from the stables until after New Year's," her husband said, reading her thoughts. "It's only a couple of weeks. The curse won't have any power after midnight on New Year's Day." Madeleine nodded, unable to speak past the lump in her throat. *Please, God, let it be so.*

Sylvia was shocked and subdued after the terrible birthday meal. For a day or two, she was glad to remain in the house under the watchful eye of her mother and those of her brothers who still lived at home. But after Christmas, she grew restless. She was used to the freedom of outdoors. She wanted to help with the animals, play games with her brothers, visit with the neighbors. She begged and pleaded so winsomely that her parents finally relented on New Year's Eve and let her go visit her godmother under the supervision of two of her brothers, who promised to keep her away from horses.

Madeleine was frying potatoes on the kitchen stove when her second-youngest child came running into the room in a

THE WITCH'S CURSE

panic. "Mama, come quickly," he cried, almost in tears. "Sylvia tripped and fell in the driveway of the manor house. She hit her head on a stone and is hurt real bad."

Madeleine gasped, threw the frying pan—potatoes and all—into the stone hearth where it would cause no harm, and ran out the door behind her son. This couldn't be the curse. It couldn't be. Sylvia had tripped and fallen in the driveway; she hadn't been kicked by a horse. So she couldn't die. *Please, God, let it be so.*

"How did she trip?" she gasped as she came parallel to her running son.

"Oh, Mama!" he gasped, tears streaming down his face. "Remember how it was raining last week and then it got all hot and dry? Well, the horses left deep hoof marks in the mud in the drive, and when it got hot the prints dried up all hard and solid. Sylvia tripped on one of the hoof marks, and that's why she fell."

A terrible pain shot through Madeleine's heart. She staggered and almost fell. Her son cried out in alarm and caught hold of her, easing her to the ground. Madeleine twisted away from him and vomited on the side of the road. It was her worst nightmare come true! Sylvia had been caught by the hoof of a horse. And she was dying. Madeleine could feel her dying somewhere in the back of her soul where she held all her children close to her.

"Mama, Mama, are you all right?" gasped her son. "Please be all right." He sounded like a little boy again, and his fear pierced the shadows gathering inside her head. She sat up and wiped her mouth.

"I'm all right," she whispered. "Help me up. Let's get to your sister."

They were met at the edge of the driveway by the plantation master himself, who lifted Madeleine into the saddle and rode up the mile-long driveway like the wind. They had carried Sylvia indoors, and the pale little girl lay on a yellow-silk couch, her dark curls spread over a matching pillow. She was barely breathing.

Madeleine fell to her knees beside her daughter, tears streaming down her face.

"We sent for the doctor," wept her godmother. "But I think she broke her neck. Oh, Madeleine, I'm so sorry."

At that moment, little Sylvia opened her lovely eyes and looked up at her mother. She tried to speak, but the words died in her throat before she could utter them. She took a breath and tiny bubbles formed at the sides of her mouth. Her little face wrinkled in distress at her inability to speak. Finally she managed to form a word with her lips: "Mama." And then she died.

The witch's curse had come true.

25

Initiation

MIAMI

I boarded the bus in Miami, resigned to a long and boring crosstown trip. The bus was a local and my stop practically the last one. I stared moodily out at the rainy city around me as a middle-aged man with a haggard face and a worn-out business suit plopped into the seat beside me and shoved a briefcase underneath it.

"Are you a student?" he asked me as the bus lurched into heavy rush-hour traffic.

"Yes," I said shortly, not wanting to talk. I had a lot on my mind. My girlfriend had broken up with me over lunch this afternoon, and I wanted to brood about it.

"I was in college once, a long time ago now," the man mused, leaning back against the seat and staring around at the crowd in the bus. It was a varied lot, from a mother of three to men in business attire to teenagers absorbed in their cell phones. "Used to belong to a fraternity. Do you belong to a fraternity?" he asked, voice and eyes suddenly sharp. The intensity with which he asked the question made me nervous.

"No, sir," I said. "I don't have time. I'm pre-med and have a lot of studying to do to get into grad school."

"Good," said the stranger, relaxing again. "Never join a fraternity, son. They're no good. My fraternity had a brutal initiation rite. They'd take candidates out to a ruin of a house outside town that they said was haunted. They'd tie the fellows up and leave them there all night with the ghosts. Nasty."

"If you believe in ghosts," I said dryly. I didn't. I am a man of science, and I believe what science can prove. That went for religion as well as ghosts. Still, if I had been a praying man, I would have started right about then. This fellow with his intense manner and too-bright eyes was making me nervous.

"Me, I made it through initiation all right. But a bloke who joined the next year didn't fare so well. All the creaking and moaning in that house, hour after hour, well it turned his brain. About two in the morning, he started screaming. He ripped out of the ropes tying him down as if they were made of spaghetti and turned on the two fellows who were tied up with him. He killed them both with the Swiss Army knife he kept in his pocket. Then he hung himself. It was a bloody mess, and I mean that literally, son."

He looked at me with his too-bright eyes, and I squirmed a bit, wondering if I should make an excuse and get off at the next stop. This guy was creeping me out.

"Happened on the third of December. I remember the date well," the stranger continued, turning his attention across the aisle to a pretty teenage girl who was rapidly texting on her phone. "Nobody in the fraternity could forget it. But it didn't end with the haunted house. No indeed. On December 3 the next year, one of the fraternity fellows who was responsible for the initiation of the crazy boy went crazy himself and shot his wife. It made the news. The next year, another one of that group flipped out and tried to run down his friends with his car. This also happened on December 3."

"That's terrible," I said, edging my body closer to the window. I was definitely getting off at the next stop—and wished the bus driver would hurry up and get us there.

"A year passed without incident," the man went on, turning his bright gaze away from the girl to study the mother and her three children. "Eight out of the ten or so boys who participated in the fatal initiation all graduated from college that year. Then one of them popped up on the news when he killed himself and his family on December 3."

Hurry up, bus driver, I thought, pushing my foot against the floor as if it were the accelerator. *Hurry up!*

"The next year, another former frat brother went crazy and drove his car off a bridge," the stranger continued, fiddling restlessly with the buttons on his worn gray business suit, his too-bright eyes resting on a red-haired businessman speaking animatedly into a cell phone. "And the following year one of the graduated frat brothers who joined the Army tried to shoot up the men serving in his platoon. Both events happened on December 3."

"Not good," I said at random, barely registering what I said, I was so jittery.

"Next year it was arson. Then murder again. Then it was suicide. And last year a former frat brother bombed a building in Chicago. All the tragedies happened on December 3, the same day the initiate went crazy all those years ago. It was like some kind of curse was killing off the men responsible for his death," the stranger said. "There's only one man left of that group now. Only one."

INITIATION

We were approaching the next bus stop, and not a minute too soon to my mind. As the bus slowed, a woman leaned forward from the seat behind us and said, "Excuse me, sir," to the stranger riding beside me. "Do you happen to know the date?" She waved her checkbook at him in silent explanation for the question.

"Why yes, ma'am, I do," he said as I grabbed my backpack from underneath my seat and prepared to rise. "It's December 3."

He smiled as he said it. Then he reached into the inside pocket of his jacket and pulled out a gun.

Resources

Alderson, Doug. *The Ghostly Ghost Tour of St. Augustine and Other Tales from Florida's Coast.* Tallahassee, FL: Earthways Press, 2009.

Asfar, Daniel. *Ghost Stories of America.* Edmonton, AB: Ghost House Books, 2001.

_____. *Ghost Stories of Florida.* Auburn, WA: Lone Pine Publishing International, 2005.

Battle, Kemp P. *Great American Folklore.* New York: Doubleday & Company, Inc., 1986.

Botkin, B. A. (ed.). *A Treasury of American Folklore.* New York: Crown, 1944.

Branham, Amanda. *Orlando Ghosts.* Atglen, PA: Schiffer Publishing Ltd., 2009.

Brewer, J. Mason. *American Negro Folklore.* Chicago: Quadrangle Books, 1972.

Brown, D. *Legends.* Eugene, OR: Randall V. Mills Archive of Northwest Folklore at the University of Oregon, 1971.

Bruce, Alexander M. *The Folklore of Florida Southern College.* Chula Vista, CA: Aventine Press, LLC, 2003.

Bruce, Annette J. *More Tellable Cracker Tales.* Sarasota, FL: Pineapple Press, Inc., 2002.

_____. *Tellable Cracker Tales.* Sarasota, FL: Pineapple Press, Inc., 1996.

Bruce, Annette J., and J. Stephen Brooks. *Sandspun: Florida Tales by Florida Tellers.* Sarasota, FL: Pineapple Press, Inc., 2001.

Brunvand, Jan Harold. *The Choking Doberman and Other Urban Legends.* New York: W. W. Norton, 1984.

_____. *The Vanishing Hitchhiker.* New York: W. W. Norton, 1981.

Carlson, Charlie. *Weird Florida.* New York: Sterling Publishing Co., Inc., 2005.

Casey, Matthew Sean. *Strange Key West.* Key West, FL: Phantom Press, 2003.

Clearfield, Dylan. *Floridaland Ghosts.* Holt, MI: Thunder Bay Press, 2000.

Coffin, Tristram. P., and Hennig Cohen (eds.). *Folklore in America.* New York: Doubleday & AMP, 1966.

_____. *Folklore from the Working Folk of America.* New York: Doubleday, 1973.

Cohen, Daniel, and Susan Cohen. *Hauntings & Horrors.* New York: Dutton Children's Books, 2002.

Congdon, Kristin G. *Uncle Monday and Other Florida Tales.* Jackson, MS: University Press of Mississippi, 2001.

Dorson, R. M. *America in Legend.* New York: Pantheon Books, 1973.

Downer, Deborah L. *Classic American Ghost Stories.* Little Rock, AR: August House Publishers, Inc., 1990.

Easley, Nicole Carlson. *Hauntings in Florida's Panhandle.* Atglen, PA: Schiffer Publishing Ltd., 2009.

Editors of Life. *The Life Treasury of American Folklore.* New York: Time Inc., 1961.

Erdoes, Richard, and Alfonso Ortiz. *American Indian Myths and Legends.* New York: Pantheon Books, 1984.

Flanagan, J. T., and A. P. Hudson. *The American Folk Reader.* New York: A. S. Barnes & Co., 1958.

Harvey, Karen. *Oldest Ghosts: St. Augustine Haunts.* Sarasota, FL: Pineapple Press, Inc., 2000.

Hauck, Dennis William. *Haunted Places: The National Directory.* New York: Penguin Books, 1994.

Jenkins, Greg. *Florida's Ghostly Legends and Haunted Folklore,* Vol. 1. Sarasota, FL: Pineapple Press, Inc., 2005.

_____. *Florida's Ghostly Legends and Haunted Folklore,* Vol. 2. Sarasota, FL: Pineapple Press, Inc., 2005.

_____. *Florida's Ghostly Legends and Haunted Folklore,* Vol. 3. Sarasota, FL: Pineapple Press, Inc., 2007.

Jones, Robert R. *Florida Ghost Stories.* Sarasota, FL: Pineapple Press, Inc., 2008.

Lamme, Vernon. *Florida Lore Not Found in the History Books.* Boynton Beach, FL: Star Publishing Company, Inc., 1973.

_____. *More Florida Lore Not Found in the History Books.* Boynton Beach, FL: Star Publishing Company, Inc., 1978.

Lapham, Dave. *Ancient City Hauntings: More Ghosts of St. Augustine.* Sarasota, FL: Pineapple Press, Inc., 2004.

_____. *Ghosts of St. Augustine.* Sarasota, FL: Pineapple Press, Inc., 1997.

Leach, M. *The Rainbow Book of American Folk Tales and Legends.* New York: The World Publishing Co., 1958.

Leeming, David, and Jake Pagey. *Myths, Legends, & Folktales of America.* New York: Oxford University Press, 1999.

Martin, C. Lee. *Florida Ghosts & Pirates.* Atglen, PA: Schiffer Publishing Ltd., 2008.

Moore, Joyce Elson. *Haunt Hunter's Guide to Florida.* Sarasota, FL: Pineapple Press, Inc., 1998.

Norman, Michael, and Beth Scott. *Historic Haunted America*. New York: Tor Books, 1995.

Patterson, Bob. *Forgotten Tales of Florida*. Charleston, SC: The History Press, 2009.

Peck, Catherine (ed.). *A Treasury of North American Folk Tales*. New York: W. W. Norton, 1998.

Polley, J. (ed.). *American Folklore and Legend*. New York: Reader's Digest Association, 1978.

Powell, Jack. *Haunting Sunshine: Ghostly Tales from Florida's Shadows*. Sarasota, FL: Pineapple Press, Inc., 2001.

Reaver, J. Russell. *Florida Folktales*. Gainesville, FL: University of Florida Press, 1987.

Reevy, Tony. *Ghost Train!* Lynchburg, VA: TLC Publishing, 1998.

Rule, Leslie. *Coast to Coast Ghosts*. Kansas City, KS: Andrews McMeel Publishing, 2001.

Schwartz, Alvin. *Scary Stories to Tell in the Dark*. New York: Harper Collins, 1981.

Skinner, Charles M. *American Myths and Legends*, Vol. 1. Philadelphia: J. B. Lippincott, 1903.

_____. *Myths and Legends of Our Own Land*, Vols. 1 & 2. Philadelphia: J. B. Lippincott, 1896.

Sloan, David L. *Ghosts of Key West*. Key West, FL: Phantom Press, 1998.

_____. *Haunted Key West*. Key West, FL: Phantom Press, 2003.

Smith, Dusty. *Haunted Daytona Beach*. Charleston, SC: Haunted America, 2007.

_____. *Haunted Deland and the Ghosts of West Volusia County*. Charleston, SC: Haunted America, 2008.

Spence, Lewis. *North American Indians: Myths and Legends Series.* London: Bracken Books, 1985.

Stavely, John F. *Ghosts and Gravestones in St. Augustine Florida.* St. Augustine, FL: Historic Tours of America, Inc., 2005.

Thuma, Cynthia, and Catherine Lower. *Haunted Florida.* Mechanicsburg, PA: Stackpole Books, 2008.

Whitehead, David W. Field *Guide to Haunted Orlando.* Florida: Self-published, 2008.

Zeitlin, Steven J., Amy J. Kotkin, and Holly Cutting Baker. *A Celebration of American Family Folklore.* New York: Pantheon Books, 1982.

From *Spooky Washington,*
also now available from GPP

At the Market

All day long, I'd been looking forward to a visit to Pike Place
Market. My husband wasn't that interested in shopping, but
he'd agreed to take me to the famous street market if I'd let him
go charter fishing in the Puget Sound the next day. Seemed like
a good deal to me!

We arrived after lunch at the main entrance to the
marketplace, and I gaped like a little kid at all the colors and
sounds. Even my husband got a kick out of seeing the market's
many stalls and strolling musicians, as well as every type of
product you could imagine hanging in doors and windows.
Hawkers shouted out their wares to passersby. Smells of flour
and cinnamon and newly baked bread wafted by on the wind,
causing my nostrils to twitch and my husband to disappear. I
was just getting worried when he reappeared with two fresh-
baked cinnamon rolls in his hands.

We munched happily as we strolled through the crowds, as bright and colorful as the goods being sold. It was a lovely, sunny day, unusual in Seattle, where clouds and rain tend to dominate the weather. My husband pulled me into a nearby park to look at the totem poles standing proudly overlooking the sound. Then I pulled him back into the marketplace to search for the source of the wonderful flower bouquets being carried in the arms of many passing shoppers. My husband's pretty swift on the uptake, and a few minutes later I was happily strolling along with my own flower masterpiece cradled in my arms.

At this point in our meanderings, we hit a solid wall of people; far too many to be moving through the narrow space between the stalls. I stayed close to my husband as I was buffeted from side-to-side by passing men, women, and children. I got an elbow in the ribs at one point, and a very rude young person cursed at me when I stepped in his way. Then someone stepped on my foot with the heel of a boot just outside a jewelry stall. By the time we reached the end of the row, I was limping and cursing under my breath and as grumpy as all get-out.

My husband was in no better state. He hates crowds worse than I do. He guided me down a ramp to the lower level of the market and found a quiet corner near a gift shop where I could lurk with my flowers while he found us something to drink. My brave hero rushed back into the swirling, wall-to-wall crowd of shoppers and disappeared from view.

I pretended to browse the nearby stalls, moving slowly in my little backwater, nursing my lovely flowers and trying not to put too much weight on my throbbing foot. I wanted to get back the holiday mood I'd had when we entered the market, but it was hard to do with my side still hurting from the elbowing,

AT THE MARKET

and my temper still red-hot from the young man's cursing. If he'd been my son, he'd have ended up in his room for being so rude to an adult.

As I stood stewing, my eyes were caught by a tall, almost ethereal figure walking down the corridor in my direction. She was a striking Native American woman with long, dark braids reaching to her waist and a lovely native basket in her hands. She wore a shimmering dress that at first I took to be white, then realized was pink. Or was it lavender? It swirled gracefully around her, covered by an old shawl that had been lovingly preserved. It was the serenity of the woman's countenance amidst the chaos of the marketplace that caught my eye. Strangely, no one else in the crowded hallway seemed to notice her. Their eyes swerved away from her, though they unconsciously made way for her as she passed. She seemed to be part of the environment without actually interacting with it, and she looked neither left nor right as she walked the hallway.

The maiden passed right in front of me at that moment, and I realized two things at once. First, I saw that she was glowing with a faint, white light. Second, I realized that I could see the stall on the other side of the hall right through her body. My mouth dropped open so far I felt my jaw pop, and goose bumps ran up the length of my arms under their flowery burden.

A moment later, the ghostly maiden turned and walked right through a wall, vanishing before my eyes. Chills rippled underneath my skin, and I started shaking. I wasn't afraid. It was impossible to be afraid of someone so serene. But I felt horribly uneasy and distressed at the sight of something so . . . unnatural.

At that moment my husband appeared, holding two cold cans of soda. "Come on, honey, I found us a place to sit!" He caught my arm with his free hand and guided me out of the marketplace to a quiet bench overlooking the sound. He must have felt me shaking, because he kept peering anxiously down at me as we walked. Once we were seated, with the huge bouquet between us on the cool stone bench, and I'd had a few calming sips of soda, he asked me what was wrong. I told him at once about seeing the ghost of the Native American woman in the marketplace. I've always made it my policy to tell my husband everything that was happening in my life, and I wasn't about to make an exception now—even though he probably wouldn't believe me. Anyway, what I'd seen was so amazing and so surreal that I had to talk about it!

"It was so strange, seeing a ghost in a crowded hallway. And no one else seemed to notice her at all," I concluded. "Maybe I imagined the whole thing."

To my surprise, my husband shook his head. "I don't think you imagined it," he said. "Your story dovetails nicely with some rumors I've heard recently about Pike Place Market."

My eyes popped. "It does?"

"Yes, it does," he said, patting my hand comfortingly. "The ghost of an Indian maiden has been seen walking these hallways for decades. Sometimes she appears in the stalls, sometimes she walks through walls, and sometimes she wanders the hallways with a basket in her hands. Some people think she's the ghost of Princess Angeline, the daughter of Chief Seattle, who used to live in this city. Others think she was one of the women who sold baskets in the marketplace when it first opened. No one knows why her spirit still appears here. But you're not the first to have seen her. And you probably won't be the last!"

189

I sighed a little in relief, grateful that he believed my story and that I had some sort of explanation for what I'd seen. I rubbed the pink petals of a peony between my thumb and forefinger, enjoying the satiny texture of the flower as we sat in silence for a few minutes, pondering the imponderable. Finally, I shook myself all over, stood up, and picked up my flowers.

"Well, I guess I got my money's worth out of this visit to the market," I said.

"You sure did! Cinnamon rolls, soda pop, flowers, and a ghost," my husband said with a grin. "Come on, let's go get some dinner!"

Grabbing my free hand, he laced his fingers through mine and led me away from the supernatural and into the golden light of a late Seattle afternoon in spring.

About the Author

S. E. Schlosser has been telling stories since she was a child, when games of "let's pretend" quickly built themselves into full-length tales acted out with friends. A graduate of Houghton College, the Institute of Children's Literature, and Rutgers University, she created and maintains the award-winning Web site Americanfolklore.net, where she shares a wealth of stories from all fifty states, some dating back to the origins of America. Sandy spends much of her time answering questions from visitors to the site. Many of her favorite e-mails come from other folklorists who delight in practicing the old tradition of who can tell the tallest tale.

About the Illustrator

Artist Paul Hoffman trained in painting and printmaking, with his first extensive illustration work on assignment in Egypt, drawing ancient wall reliefs for the University of Chicago. His work graces books of many genres—children's titles, textbooks, short story collections, natural history volumes, and numerous cookbooks. For *Spooky Florida*, he employed a scratchboard technique and an active imagination.

Printed in Great Britain
by Amazon

41237172R00118